MW00808253

NO FEAR

Beowulf

The Canterbury Tales

The Scarlett Letter

NO FEAR SHAKESPEARE

Antony and Cleopatra

As You Like It

The Comedy of Errors

Coriolanus

Hamlet

Henry IV, Parts One and Two

Henry V

Julius Caesar

King Lear

Macbeth

Measure for Measure

The Merchant of Venice

A Midsummer Night's Dream

Much Ado About Nothing

Othello

Richard II

Richard III

Romeo and Juliet

Sonnets

The Taming of the Shrew

The Tempest

The Winter's Tale

Twelfth Night

Two Gentlemen of Verona

NO FEAR

THE
U.S. CONSTITUTION
AND
OTHER IMPORTANT
AMERICAN DOCUMENTS

*sparknotes

ISBN 978-1-4549-2808-9

Distributed in Canada by Sterling Publishing Co., Inc.
c/o Canadian Manda Group, 664 Annette Street
Toronto, Ontario, M6S 2C8, Canada
Distributed in the United Kingdom by GMC Distribution Services
Castle Place, 166 High Street, Lewes, East Sussex, BN7 1XU, England
Distributed in Australia by NewSouth Books
45 Beach Street, Coogee, NSW 2034, Australia

For information about custom editions, special sales, and premium
and corporate purchases, please contact Sterling Special Sales at
800-805-5489 or specialsales@sterlingpublishing.com.

Manufactured in the United States of America

Lot #:
2 4 6 8 10 9 7 5 3 1
12/17

sterlingpublishing.com
sparknotes.com

CONTENTS

INTRODUCTION

The Declaration of Independence, the Articles of Confederation, the Constitution, and the Gettysburg Address have all shaped America into the nation it is today. Each of these documents served a different function and altered the way Americans perceive their country. The Declaration of Independence separated the thirteen colonies from Great Britain and outlined the philosophical ideals of the new nation when it was written in 1776. A few years later, the Articles of Confederation established the first national government for the newly independent states. The Constitution replaced the Articles twelve years later and created a stronger system of government that embodied the ideals of the Declaration and remains to this day. And finally, Abraham Lincoln's Gettysburg Address, delivered in 1863 during the Civil War, characterized America as a beacon of hope and freedom for the rest of humanity.

The original text of the four documents is organized and very specific. The structure of the Constitution, for example, clarifies how the government should function. It divides the government into three parts, all relatively equal in power so that no one branch can overpower the others. At the same time, the writers of the Constitution knew that they wouldn't be able to predict the future challenges the nation would face, such as the Cold War, abortion, or electronic eavesdropping. Therefore, they made certain that the Constitution was flexible enough to allow the government to address any of these unpredictable issues. Parts of the Constitution are relatively vague, such as the Elastic Clause in Article I, Section 8, for example, which gives Congress the power to "make all laws which shall be necessary and proper" to uphold the Constitution; it's a clause that allows Congress to pass new laws as needed. And, of course, amendments can always be added to the Constitution to make sure that some changes will be permanent. For this reason, most historians refer to the Constitution as a living document, a document whose meaning changes with time as the nation faces new challenges.

Unlike other companion volumes on the Constitution, this book doesn't interpret the Constitution or the other documents. Instead, it presents the original texts of the Declaration of Independence, the Articles of Confederation, the Constitution, and the Gettysburg Address side by side with modern translations that anyone can understand. Sometimes the translations are purposefully vague, especially for parts of the Constitution that the Founding Fathers wanted to be vague, such as the Elastic Clause. Modernizing the language without altering the intent in this way highlights the genius (or inadequacy, in the case of the Articles) of the documents and allows readers to draw their own conclusions.

THE
DECLARATION
OF
INDEPENDENCE

When Thomas Jefferson was selected in 1776 to write the Declaration of Independence, his job was to convince people all over the world that the colonies had the right to rebel against Great Britain. Jefferson strived to keep the document relatively short so the message would be powerful and to the point. His efforts were successful. In just a few paragraphs, Jefferson rallied the American people with damning evidence against Great Britain and King George III. In fact, Jefferson constructed a solid argument by listing King George III's wrongdoings in the same way one would present evidence in a trial.

Jefferson's most important argument was that governments derive their power from the people, an idea inspired by the writings of Enlightenment philosophers Jean Jacques Rousseau and Thomas Paine, among others. Both men believed that the people and their government had an unspoken agreement called a social contract. According to this agreement, the people had the right to create a new government when the old one no longer protected their interests. This idea was radical because, at the time, Europeans believed in the divine right of kings— that God wanted kings to rule and gave them their power.

The Declaration of Independence introduced the idea of holding monarchies and governments accountable to the people.

Jefferson's phrase "all men are created equal" formed a bond between colonists from all classes and walks of life. Colonists also agreed that all men had certain rights that no one could take away, including the rights to "Life, Liberty, and the pursuit of Happiness." Many believed that these seven words made America different from Europe and the rest of the world because Americans could always strive to improve their lives regardless of their class, religion, and, eventually, gender and race. Ultimately, Jefferson described what would eventually be known as the American Dream.

THE DECLARATION OF INDEPENDENCE

*IN CONGRESS, JULY 4, 1776. The unanimous
Declaration of the thirteen united States of America*

When in the Course of human Events, it becomes necessary for one People to dissolve the Political Bands which have connected them with another, and to assume among the Powers of the Earth, the separate and equal Station to which the Laws of Nature and of Nature's God entitle them, a decent Respect to the Opinions of Mankind requires that they should declare the causes which impel them to the Separation.

We hold these truths to be self-evident, that all Men are created equal, that they are endowed by their Creator with certain unalienable Rights, that among these are Life, Liberty and the pursuit of Happiness.—That to secure these Rights, Governments are instituted among Men, deriving their just powers from the consent of the Governed, that whenever any Form of Government becomes destructive of these ends, it is the Right of the People to alter or to abolish it, and to institute new Government, laying its Foundation on such Principles and organizing its Powers in such Form, as to them shall seem most likely to effect their Safety and Happiness. Prudence, indeed, will dictate that Governments long established should not be changed for light and transient Causes; and accordingly all Experience hath shewn, that Mankind are more disposed to suffer, while Evils are sufferable, than to right themselves by abolishing

THE DECLARATION OF INDEPENDENCE

Thomas Jefferson, the third president of the United States, wrote the Declaration of Independence when he was thirty-two years old.

The unanimous declaration of the thirteen states that make up the United States of America

Sometimes, one group of people must cut off the political ties that connect them to another group of people and claim the independence and equality that the laws of nature and the Creator guarantee. When doing so, they must explain their reasons for declaring independence in order to respect all mankind in general.

In his first draft, Jefferson wrote that people were fundamentally equal regardless of race too, but colonial leaders from the South cut this from the final version.

The Declaration is a secular document, which means it has nothing to do with religion. Because Jefferson feared people would interpret the word God to mean the God of the Bible, he used generic words such as Nature's God, Creator, and Supreme Judge.

We believe it to be undeniably true that all men are created equal and are given certain unalienable rights by their Creator—rights that can't be taken away. These rights include the right to life, the right to liberty, and the right to try to be happy. People create governments to protect these rights, and governments get their power from the people they govern. Whenever any kind of government fails to protect these rights, the people have the right to change it or get rid of it and to create a new government as they see fit to best promote their safety and happiness. Of course, governments that have existed for a long time shouldn't be changed for insignificant reasons. History shows that people tend to endure hardships, as long as those hardships are manageable, rather than eliminate the

the Forms to which they are accustomed. But when a long Train of Abuses and Usurpations, pursuing invariably the same Object, evinces a Design to reduce them under absolute Despotism, it is their Right, it is their Duty, to throw off such Government, and to provide new Guards for their future Security. Such has been the patient Sufferance of these Colonies; and such is now the Necessity which constrains them to alter their former Systems of Government. The History of the present King of Great-Britain is a History of repeated Injuries and Usurpations, all having in direct Object the Establishment of an absolute Tyranny over these States. To prove this, let Facts be submitted to a candid World.

He has refuted his Assent to Laws, the most wholesome and necessary for the public Good.

He has forbidden his Governors to pass Laws of immediate and pressing Importance, unless suspended in their Operation till his Assent should be obtained; and when so suspended, he has utterly neglected to attend to them.

He has refused to pass other Laws for the Accommodation of large Districts of People, unless those People would relinquish the Right of Representation in the Legislature, a Right inestimable to them, and formidable to Tyrants only.

He has called together Legislative Bodies at Places unusual, uncomfortable, and distant from the Depository of their public Records, for the sole Purpose of fatiguing them into Compliance with his Measures.

He has dissolved Representative Houses repeatedly, for opposing with manly Firmness his Invasions on the Rights of the People.

forms of government that they're familiar with. But when a tyrannical government repeatedly abuses the people, then the people have the right and duty to get rid of that government and find a new way to protect their rights. The American colonies have suffered patiently in this way for a long time, and therefore find it necessary to change their system of government. The current King of Great Britain has repeatedly mistreated the colonies like a despot. Here is factual proof for the whole world to see.

The King of Great Britain was King George III.

- The King hasn't obeyed the law, which is necessary to promote the public good.

- He has prevented Governors from passing important and urgent laws and has required them to ask his permission before doing anything. But he doesn't pay attention when they ask.

- He has refused to pass other laws for large groups of people unless they give up their right to representation in the legislature. Only tyrants would do this, because everyone is entitled to representation.

- He has told legislatures to meet at unusual and inconvenient places that are far from the places where the legislative records are kept in an effort to weaken them so that they'll do what he tells them to do.

- He has repeatedly broken up legislatures and town meetings for opposing his decisions that take away the people's rights.

He has refused for a long Time, after such Dissolutions, to cause others to be elected; whereby the Legislative Powers, incapable of Annihilation, have returned to the People at large for their exercise; the State remaining in the mean time exposed to all the Dangers of Invasion from without, and Convulsions within.

He has endeavoured to prevent the Population of these States; for that Purpose obstructing the Laws for Naturalization of Foreigners; refusing to pass others to encourage their Migrations hither, and raising the Conditions of new Appropriations of Lands.

He has obstructed the Administration of Justice, by refusing his Assent to Laws for establishing Judiciary Powers.

He has made Judges dependent on his Will alone, for the Tenure of their Offices, and the Amount and Payment of their Salaries.

He has erected a Multitude of new Offices, and sent hither Swarms of Officers to harass our People, and eat out their Substance.

He has kept among us, in Times of Peace, Standing Armies without the consent of our Legislatures.

He has affected to render the Military independent of and superior to the Civil Power.

He has combined with others to subject us to a Jurisdiction foreign to our Constitution, and unacknowledged by our Laws; giving his Assent to their Acts of pretended Legislation:

- He hasn't allowed the people to elect new Representatives after breaking up the legislatures, which has left the people without any way to make laws and at risk from both foreign and domestic dangers.

Colonists resented the Proclamation of 1763, which forbade them from settling west of the Appalachian Mountains after the French and Indian War.

- He has tried to prevent the colonies from growing. He has made it difficult for foreigners to live in the colonies legally and hasn't allowed colonists to acquire new land or move to new territories.

- He has bogged down the legal system by not approving the laws necessary to establish judicial powers.

- He has put judges' terms of office and salaries at his mercy.

- He has created many new offices and has sent great numbers of officers to harass our citizens and take away their livelihood.

Colonists resented the thousands of British troops who remained in the colonies after the French and Indian War, as well as the military occupation of Boston in the early 1770s.

- He has maintained armies throughout the colonies in times of peace without the approval of the local legislatures.

- He has tried to make the military independent of and more powerful than civilian legislatures.

- He has subjected us to laws that we don't recognize, such as laws to:

For quartering large Bodies of Armed Troops among us:

For protecting them, by a mock Trial, from Punishment for any Murders which they should commit on the Inhabitants of these States:

For cutting off our Trade with all Parts of the World:

For imposing Taxes on us without our Consent:

For depriving us, in many Cases, of the Benefits of Trial by Jury:

For transporting us beyond Seas to be tried for pretended Offences:

For abolishing the free System of English Laws in a neighbouring Province, establishing therein an arbitrary Government, and enlarging its Boundaries, so as to render it at once an Example and fit Instrument for introducing the same absolute Rule into these Colonies:

For taking away our Charters, abolishing our most valuable Laws, and altering fundamentally the Forms of our Governments:

For suspending our own Legislatures, and declaring themselves invested with Power to legislate for us in all Cases whatsoever.

He has abdicated Government here, by declaring us out of his Protection and waging War against us.

He has plundered our Seas, ravaged our Coasts, burnt our Towns, and destroyed the Lives of our People.

- House large numbers of troops among us

- Set up fake courts to protect those troops from punishment for murdering colonists

- Interfere with our trade with other countries

- Tax us without our permission

- Rob us of the right to trial by jury in many cases

- Take us overseas to stand trial for crimes we didn't commit

- Abolish laws in a nearby province, create an arbitrary government there, stretch its boundaries, and introduce the same unjust rule that exists in the colonies

- Take away our charters as royal colonies, destroy valuable laws, and change the basic form of our government

- Disband our legislatures and give himself the authority to make laws for us at his whim

• He has failed to fulfill his governing responsibilities by not protecting us and waging war against us.

• He has pirated our seas, demolished our coasts, burned our towns, and ruined the lives of our people.

He is, at this Time, transporting large Armies of foreign Mercenaries to compleat the Works of Death, Desolation, and Tyranny, already begun with circumstances of Cruelty and Perfidy, scarcely paralleled in the most barbarous Ages, and totally unworthy the Head of a civilized Nation.

He has constrained our fellow Citizens taken Captive on the high Seas to bear Arms against their Country, to become the Executioners of their Friends and Brethren, or to fall themselves by their Hands.

He has excited domestic Insurrections amongst us, and has endeavoured to bring on the Inhabitants of our Frontiers, the merciless Indian Savages, whose known Rule of Warfare, is an undistinguished Destruction of all Ages, Sexes and Conditions.

In every stage of these Oppressions we have Petitioned for Redress in the most humble Terms: Our repeated Petitions have been answered only by repeated Injury. A Prince, whose Character is thus marked by every act which may define a Tyrant, is unfit to be the Ruler of a free People.

Nor have we been wanting in Attentions to our British Brethren. We have warned them from Time to Time of attempts by their Legislature to extend an unwarrantable Jurisdiction over us. We have reminded them of the Circumstances of our Emigration and Settlement here. We have appealed to their native Justice and Magnanimity, and we have conjured them by the Ties of our common Kindred to disavow these Usurpations, which, would inevitably interrupt our Connections and Correspondence. They too have been deaf to the Voice of Justice and of Consanguinity. We must, therefore, acquiesce in the Necessity, which denounces our Separation, and hold them, as we hold the rest of Mankind, Enemies in War, in Peace, Friends.

- He is presently bringing large armies of foreign soldiers to kill, destroy, and subdue our people in such a way that was unmatched in even the most barbaric times in history. These actions are unworthy of the leader of a civilized nation.

Colonists resented the royal navy impressing American sailors, which means forcing them into military service on British ships.

- He has captured colonists on ships at sea and forced them to fight against the colonies and kill their fellow colonists or be killed themselves.

- He has encouraged revolutions among us and sought to pit Native American savages against frontier settlers, even though Native Americans are known to kill everyone, including women, children, and the elderly.

We have humbly asked that these wrongs be corrected, but our requests have been answered with continued tyranny. If a ruler is capable of acting only as a tyrant, then he's unfit to rule a free people.

We have also tried warning the British people. From time to time, we have informed them that their government was trying to control us too much. We have reminded them why we left Great Britain and settled here. We have appealed to their sense of justice and kindness, and we have reminded them of our common ancestry so as not to disrupt our good relations. But they haven't listened to us. It's therefore necessary to think of the British people not as our brethren, but as any other person: friends during peace, but enemies during war.

We, therefore, the Representatives of the UNITED STATES OF AMERICA, in General Congress, Assembled, appealing to the Supreme Judge of the World for the Rectitude of our Intentions, do, in the Name, and by Authority of the good People of these Colonies, solemnly Publish and Declare, That these United Colonies are, and of Right ought to be, FREE AND INDEPENDENT STATES; that they are absolved from all Allegiance to the British Crown, and that all political Connection between them and the State of Great-Britain, is and ought to be totally dissolved; and that as FREE AND INDEPENDENT STATES, they have full Power to levy War, conclude Peace, contract Alliances, establish Commerce, and to do all other Acts and Things which INDEPENDENT STATES may of right do. And for the support of this Declaration, with a firm Reliance on the Protection of divine Providence, we mutually pledge to each other our Lives, our Fortunes, and our sacred Honor.

—John Hancock

NEW HAMPSHIRE
Josiah Bartlett; William Whipple; Matthew Thornton

MASSACHUSETTS
John Hancock; Samuel Adams; John Adams; Robert Treat Paine; Elbridge Gerry

RHODE ISLAND
Stephen Hopkins; William Ellery

CONNECTICUT
Roger Sherman; Samuel Huntington; William Williams; Oliver Wolcott

So, as Representatives of the colonists and asking the Creator to accept the righteousness of our decision, we solemnly declare that these united colonies have the right to be free and independent. The colonies are freed from their obligation of loyalty to the King, and there is no longer any political connection between the colonies and Great Britain. Being free and independent, the new states now have the powers to declare war, make peace, trade, and do everything else that independent countries have the right to do. And in support of this declaration, relying on the protection of the Creator, we pledge to each other our lives, our wealth, and our sacred honor.

John Hancock

NEW HAMPSHIRE
Josiah Bartlett; William Whipple; Matthew Thornton

MASSACHUSETTS
John Hancock; Samuel Adams; John Adams; Robert Treat Paine; Elbridge Gerry

RHODE ISLAND
Stephen Hopkins; William Ellery

CONNECTICUT
Roger Sherman; Samuel Huntington; William Williams; Oliver Wolcott

NEW YORK
William Floyd; Philip Livingston; Francis Lewis; Lewis Morris

NEW JERSEY
Richard Stockton; John Witherspoon; Francis Hopkinson; John Hart; Abraham Clark

PENNSYLVANIA
Robert Morris; Benjamin Rush; Benjamin Franklin; John Morton; George Clymer; James Smith; George Taylor; James Wilson; George Ross

DELAWARE
Caesar Rodney; George Read; Thomas McKean

MARYLAND
Samuel Chase; William Paca; Thomas Stone; Charles Carroll of Carrollton

VIRGINIA
George Wythe; Richard Henry Lee; Thomas Jefferson; Benjamin Harrison; Thomas Nelson, Jr.; Francis Lightfoot Lee; Carter Braxton

NORTH CAROLINA
William Hooper; Joseph Hewes; John Penn

SOUTH CAROLINA
Edward Rutledge; Thomas Heyward, Jr.; Thomas Lynch, Jr.; Arthur Middleton

GEORGIA
Button Gwinnett; Lyman Hall; George Walton

NEW YORK
William Floyd; Philip Livingston; Francis Lewis; Lewis Morris

NEW JERSEY
Richard Stockton; John Witherspoon; Francis Hopkinson; John Hart; Abraham Clark

PENNSYLVANIA
Robert Morris; Benjamin Rush; Benjamin Franklin; John Morton; George Clymer; James Smith; George Taylor; James Wilson; George Ross

DELAWARE
Caesar Rodney; George Read; Thomas McKean

MARYLAND
Samuel Chase; William Paca; Thomas Stone; Charles Carroll of Carrollton

VIRGINIA
George Wythe; Richard Henry Lee; Thomas Jefferson; Benjamin Harrison; Thomas Nelson, Jr.; Francis Lightfoot Lee; Carter Braxton

NORTH CAROLINA
William Hooper; Joseph Hewes; John Penn

SOUTH CAROLINA
Edward Rutledge; Thomas Heyward, Jr.; Thomas Lynch, Jr.; Arthur Middleton

GEORGIA
Button Gwinnett; Lyman Hall; George Walton

THE
ARTICLES OF
CONFEDERATION

The Articles of Confederation was one of the world's first written constitutions that clearly outlined the rights, duties, and powers of the government and the people.

In 1777, colonial leaders wrote the Articles to create a government for the new country. The new government consisted of a national Congress composed of representatives from each of the states. Each state had one vote in Congress, and decisions were usually made by majority rule.

The Articles of Confederation gave Congress limited, specific powers over the states. The Founding Fathers purposefully made Congress weak because they feared strong central governments. Instead, Congress would merely supervise the states and keep them bound together for the common good. Under the Articles, states had more powers than they do today and were treated more like independent countries than provinces. The early United States was more a confederation of loosely allied states than a single, unified country.

This system of government ultimately failed because the Articles of Confederation made Congress *too* weak. The individual states had too much power, looked out for their own interests, and often refused to work together. Worse, Congress had no power to punish wayward states or to collect taxes. With the economy failing and inflation skyrocketing, many poor farmers began rebelling against their state governments. Worried that their new country would collapse after only a little more than a decade, some leading statesmen organized a meeting in 1787 to discuss revising the Articles or even replacing them with another document to create a stronger government.

THE ARTICLES OF CONFEDERATION

Agreed to by Congress November 15, 1777; ratified and in force, March 1, 1781.

PREAMBLE

To all to whom these Presents shall come, we the under-signed Delegates of the States affixed to our Names send greeting. The Articles of Confederation and Perpetual Union Between the States of New Hampshire, Massachusetts bay Rhode Island and Providence Plantations, Connecticut, New York, New Jersey, Pennsylvania, Delaware, Maryland, Virginia, North Carolina, South Carolina and Georgia.

ARTICLE I

The Stile of this Confederacy shall be "The United States of America".

ARTICLE II

Each state retains its sovereignty, freedom, and independence, and every power, jurisdiction, and right, which is not by this Confederation expressly delegated to the United States, in Congress assembled.

ARTICLE III

The said States hereby severally enter into a firm league of friendship with each other, for their common defense, the security of their liberties, and their mutual and general welfare,

THE ARTICLES OF CONFEDERATION

Approved by Congress on November 15, 1777, and ratified and enacted on March 1, 1781.

PREAMBLE: INTRODUCTION

We, the Representatives of the states and signers of this document, greet the people who read these articles. These are the Articles of Confederation to create a permanent union between the states of New Hampshire, Massachusetts Bay, Rhode Island and Providence Plantations, Connecticut, New York, New Jersey, Pennsylvania, Delaware, Maryland, Virginia, North Carolina, South Carolina, and Georgia.

ARTICLE 1: NAME

The name of this confederacy will be *The United States of America.*

A confederacy is a group of loosely united governments, in this case, states. Under the Articles of Confederation, states were more like allied, independent countries than provinces under a single national government.

ARTICLE 2: FREEDOM AND INDEPENDENCE

Each state keeps its independence and freedom as well as all powers, legal jurisdictions, and rights not given exclusively to the Congress of the United States by these articles.

ARTICLE 3: UNION

These states will form a league of friendship with each other to provide for their common defense, the security of their freedoms, and their collective well-being.

binding themselves to assist each other, against all force offered to, or attacks made upon them, or any of them, on account of religion, sovereignty, trade, or any other pretense whatever.

ARTICLE IV

The better to secure and perpetuate mutual friendship and intercourse among the people of the different States in this Union, the free inhabitants of each of these States, paupers, vagabonds, and fugitives from justice excepted, shall be entitled to all privileges and immunities of free citizens in the several States; and the people of each State shall free ingress and regress to and from any other State, and shall enjoy therein all the privileges of trade and commerce, subject to the same duties, impositions, and restrictions as the inhabitants thereof respectively, provided that such restrictions shall not extend so far as to prevent the removal of property imported into any State, to any other State, of which the owner is an inhabitant; provided also that no imposition, duties or restriction shall be laid by any State, on the property of the United States, or either of them.

If any person guilty of, or charged with, treason, felony, or other high misdemeanor in any State, shall flee from justice, and be found in any of the United States, he shall, upon demand of the Governor or executive power of the State from which he fled, be delivered up and removed to the State having jurisdiction of his offense.

Full faith and credit shall be given in each of these States to the records, acts, and judicial proceedings of the courts and magistrates of every other State.

ARTICLE V

For the most convenient management of the general interests of the United States, delegates shall be annually

As members of this confederation, they agree to defend each other in the event of attacks made against any of them because of religion, independence, trade, or any other reason.

ARTICLE 4: BASIC RIGHTS OF THE PEOPLE

The free inhabitants of each state, except for poor people who depend on charity, tramps, and fugitives from the law, will have the same privileges and rights of citizens in every other state in order to maintain good relations between the people of different states. The people of each state will be allowed to enter and exit every other state freely, will have the same rules of trade and business including taxes and restrictions, and can move their private property between states. States can't place taxes or restrictions on the United States or any of the other member states.

Any person charged with or found guilty of treason, series crimes, or other lesser crimes who flees from justice to another state will be returned to the state from which he fled at the Governor's request.

Each state must respect the public records, laws, and court rulings of every other state.

ARTICLE 5: CONGRESS

To manage the general affairs of the United States, State legislatures will appoint Representatives to appointed in such manner as the legislatures of each State shall direct, to meet in Congress on the first Monday in November, in every year, with a power reserved to each State to recall its delegates, or any of them, at any time within the year, and to send others in their stead for the remainder of the year.

No State shall be represented in Congress by less than two, nor more than seven members; and no person shall be capable of being a delegate for more than three years in any term of six years; nor shall any person, being a delegate, be capable of holding any office under the United States, for which he, or another for his benefit, receives any salary, fees or emolument of any kind.

Each State shall maintain its own delegates in a meeting of the States, and while they act as members of the committee of the States.

In determining questions in the United States in Congress assembled, each State shall have one vote.

Freedom of speech and debate in Congress shall not be impeached or questioned in any court or place out of Congress, and the members of Congress shall be protected in their persons from arrests or imprisonments, during the time of their going to and from, and attendance on Congress, except for treason, felony, or breach of the peace.

ARTICLE VI

No State, without the consent of the United States in Congress assembled, shall send any embassy to, or receive any embassy from, or enter into any conference, agreement, alliance or treaty with any King, Prince or State;

Congress every year in whatever way they see fit. These Representatives will meet on the first Monday of November of each year. States can recall and replace any or all of their Representatives at anytime during the year.

Each state will have between two and seven represen- tatives in Congress. No one can be a Representative for more than three years in any six-year period. Rep- resentatives can't hold other salaried positions in the United States government while they hold office.

Each state will send its own Representatives to meet- ings of the states and to the Committee of the States.

The Committee of the States was a group of thirteen men, one from each state, who met whenever Congress was taking a break. See Article IX, Paragraph 6.

Each state will have one vote when Congress is mak- ing decisions about the United States.

Courts can't take away Representatives' right to speak and debate freely in Congress, and Representatives don't have to answer questions outside of Congress about anything they say while speaking in Congress. With the exception of treason, other high crimes, and disturbing the peace, Representatives can't be arrested while meeting in Congress or when traveling to meet- ings of Congress.

ARTICLE 6: RESTRICTIONS

States can't send or receive ambassadors or form any agreements, alliances, or treaties with foreign rulers or other countries without the approval of Congress.

nor shall any person holding any office of profit or trust under the United States, or any of them, accept any present, emolument, office or title of any kind whatever from any King, Prince or foreign State; nor shall the United States in Congress assembled, or any of them, grant any title of nobility.

No two or more States shall enter into any treaty, confederation or alliance whatever between them, without the consent of the United States in Congress assembled, specifying accurately the purposes for which the same is to be entered into, and how long it shall continue.

No State shall lay any imposts or duties, which may interfere with any stipulations in treaties, entered into by the United States in Congress assembled, with any King, Prince or State, in pursuance of any treaties already proposed by Congress, to the courts of France and Spain.

No vessel of war shall be kept up in time of peace by any State, except such number only, as shall be deemed necessary by the United States in Congress assembled, for the defense of such State, or its trade; nor shall any body of forces be kept up by any State in time of peace, except such number only, as in the judgement of the United States in Congress assembled, shall be deemed requisite to garrison the forts necessary for the defense of such State; but every State shall always keep up a well-regulated and disciplined militia, sufficiently armed and accoutered, and shall provide and constantly have ready for use, in public stores, a due number of filed pieces and tents, and a proper quantity of arms, ammunition and camp equipage.

No State shall engage in any war without the consent of the United States in Congress assembled, unless such State be actually invaded by enemies, or shall have received certain advice of a resolution being formed by some nation of

People holding offices of the United States can't accept gifts, payments or titles from foreign rulers or other countries. The Congress of the United States can't give titles of nobility either.

States can't form any treaties, agreements, or alliances with other states without the consent of Congress and must clearly specify the duration and reason for the alliance.

States can't create any taxes that would interfere with treaties between the United States Congress and foreign rulers or other states, in accordance with the treaties with France and Spain that have already been proposed.

States can't keep any warships during peacetime, except those that Congress believes are necessary for the defense of that state or its trade. States also can't keep armies during peacetime, except those that Congress believes are necessary to operate states' defensive forts. Every state, however, must maintain a disciplined, armed militia as well as a sufficient amount of food, tents, arms, ammunition, and other camp gear that can be used at a moment's notice.

States can't fight wars without the approval of Congress, except to repel invasions, attack hostile Native

Indians to invade such State, and the danger is so imminent as not to admit of a delay till the United States in Congress assembled can be consulted; nor shall any State grant commissions to any ships or vessels of war, nor letters of marque or reprisal, except it be after a declaration of war by the United States in Congress assembled, and then only against the Kingdom or State and the subjects thereof, against which war has been so declared, and under such regulations as shall be established by the United States in Congress assembled, unless such State be infested by pirates, in which case vessels of war may be fitted out for that occasion, and kept so long as the danger shall continue, or until the United States in Congress assembled shall determine otherwise.

ARTICLE VII

When land forces are raised by any State for the common defense, all officers of or under the rank of colonel, shall be appointed by the legislature of each State respectively, by whom such forces shall be raised, or in such manner as such State shall direct, and all vacancies shall be filled up by the State which first made the appointment.

ARTICLE VIII

All charges of war, and all other expenses that shall be incurred for the common defense or general welfare, and allowed by the United States in Congress assembled, shall be defrayed out of a common treasury, which shall be supplied by the several States in proportion to the value of all land within each State, granted or surveyed for any person, as such land and the buildings and improvements thereon shall be estimated according to such mode as the United States in Congress assembled, shall from time to time direct and appoint.

The taxes for paying that proportion shall be laid and levied by the authority and direction of the legislatures of the sev-

Americans who're preparing for war, or in extreme emergencies when there is no time to consult Congress. States can't build warships or issue letters of marque to hire others to seize private property unless Congress has declared war, and then only against the country and its people against which Congress declared war. Even then, each state must obey the regulations of war that Congress has established, except when fighting pirates, in which case states may continue to arm warships until the danger is gone or until Congress says otherwise.

A letter of marque provides authorization to seize private property. Governments would often issue letters of marque to privateers—merchants, pirates, mercenaries, and other individuals—to capture enemy ships.

ARTICLE 7: MILITARY OFFICERS

States will appoint all officers with and under the rank of colonel when they raise armies for the defense of the entire country. Each state will also appoint officers to fill any vacant posts in its army.

ARTICLE 8: FINANCES

The costs of war and other expenses that add up while defending the United States, if approved of by Congress, approves will be paid from a common treasury. Each state will put money into the treasury in proportion to the value of its land. Congress will assess the value of the land from time to time using surveys or other methods it deems appropriate.

To contribute to this treasury, each state legislature will be responsible for setting and collecting taxes eral States within the time agreed upon by the United States in Congress assembled.

ARTICLE IX

The United States in Congress assembled, shall have the sole and exclusive right and power of determining on peace and war, except in the cases mentioned in the sixth article— of sending and receiving ambassadors—entering into treaties and alliances, provided that no treaty of commerce shall be made whereby the legislative power of the respective States shall be restrained from imposing such imposts and duties on foreigners, as their own people are subjected to, or from prohibiting the exportation or importation of any species of goods or commodities whatsoever—of establishing rules for deciding in all cases, what captures on land or water shall be legal, and in what manner prizes taken by land or naval forces in the service of the United States shall be divided or appropriated—of granting letters of marque and reprisal in times of peace—appointing courts for the trial of piracies and felonies committed on the high seas and establishing courts for receiving and determining finally appeals in all cases of captures, provided that no member of Congress shall be appointed a judge of any of the said courts.

The United States in Congress assembled shall also be the last resort on appeal in all disputes and differences now subsisting or that hereafter may arise between two or more States concerning boundary, jurisdiction or any other causes whatever; which authority shall always be exercised in the manner following. Whenever the legislative or executive authority or lawful agent of any State in controversy with another shall present a petition to Congress stating the matter in question and praying for a hearing, notice thereof shall be given by order of Congress to the legislative or executive authority of the other State in controversy, and a

from its citizens. States must do so within the time-frame that Congress sets.

ARTICLE 9: THE POWERS OF CONGRESS

Only Congress can declare war and make peace, except under the special circumstance outlined in Article 6 of this document. Only Congress can send and receive ambassadors and form treaties and alliances, as long as those agreements don't prevent states from taxing foreigners or from importing and exporting goods. Only Congress can decide when it's legal to seize goods on land and at sea and how to divide and distribute those items seized by the United States military. Only Congress can issue letters of marque during peaceful times. Only Congress can create courts to try people accused of piracy and high crimes at sea, and courts to hear the appeals of those individuals. Representatives to Congress can't serve as judges on these courts.

Congress will have the final say when resolving current and future arguments between states about borders, legal authority, and everything else. Congress will resolve disagreements in the following way: When a legislature, governor, or other Representative of one state asks Congress to resolve a dispute, Congress will notify the legislature, Governor, or Representative of the other state or states involved in the dispute.

day assigned for the appearance of the parties by their lawful agents, who shall then be directed to appoint by joint consent, commissioners or judges to constitute a court for hearing and determining the matter in question: but if they cannot agree, Congress shall name three persons out of each of the United States, and from the list of such persons each party shall alternately strike out one, the petitioners beginning, until the number shall be reduced to thirteen; and from that number not less than seven, nor more than nine names as Congress shall direct, shall in the presence of Congress be drawn out by lot, and the persons whose names shall be so drawn or any five of them, shall be commissioners or judges, to hear and finally determine the controversy, so always as a major part of the judges who shall hear the cause shall agree in the determination: and if either party shall neglect to attend at the day appointed, without showing reasons, which Congress shall judge sufficient, or being present shall refuse to strike, the Congress shall proceed to nominate three persons out of each State, and the secretary of Congress shall strike in behalf of such party absent or refusing; and the judgement and sentence of the court to be appointed, in the manner before prescribed, shall be final and conclusive; and if any of the parties shall refuse to submit to the authority of such court, or to appear or defend their claim or cause, the court shall nevertheless proceed to pronounce sentence, or judgement, which shall in like manner be final and decisive, the judgement or sentence and other proceedings being in either case transmitted to Congress, and lodged among the acts of Congress for the security of the parties concerned: provided that every commissioner, before he sits in judgement, shall take an oath to be administered by one of the judges of the supreme or superior court of the State, where the cause shall be tried, 'well and truly to hear and determine the matter in question, according to the best of his judgement, without favor,

Congress will set aside a day when representatives from each state will meet to choose three individuals to be judges in the case. If the Representatives can't agree on any judges, Congress will make a list with the names of three people from each state. The Representatives from the arguing states will then take turns eliminating names from the list, one by one, until only thirteen names remain. Congress will then randomly choose seven, eight, or nine people by lot from those thirteen names. At least five of the names drawn will then serve as judges to resolve the dispute. Final decisions are made by a majority vote. If Representatives from any disputing state refuse to participate or don't show up on the appointed day without a reasonable excuse, Congress will make a list of three people from each state anyway, and the Secretary of the Congress will serve as the representative of the absent state. The appointed court's decision and sentence will be final, even if the disputing states refuse to argue their case or accept the court's authority. The court's decision will be given to Congress and registered as a law of Congress for the sake of the states involved. Before serving on these courts, judges must take an oath administered by a supreme or superior court judge from the state where the trial is being held. Each judge must vow "well and truly to hear and determine the matter in question, according to the best of his judgment, without favor, affection or hope of reward."

affection or hope of reward': provided also, that no State shall be deprived of territory for the benefit of the United States.

All controversies concerning the private right of soil claimed under different grants of two or more States, whose jurisdictions as they may respect such lands, and the States which passed such grants are adjusted, the said grants or either of them being at the same time claimed to have originated antecedent to such settlement of jurisdiction, shall on the petition of either party to the Congress of the United States, be finally determined as near as may be in the same manner as is before prescribed for deciding disputes respecting territorial jurisdiction between different States.

The United States in Congress assembled shall also have the sole and exclusive right and power of regulating the alloy and value of coin struck by their own authority, or by that of the respective States—fixing the standards of weights and measures throughout the United States—regulating the trade and managing all affairs with the Indians, not members of any of the States, provided that the legislative right of any State within its own limits be not infringed or violated—establishing or regulating post offices from one State to another, throughout all the United States, and exacting such postage on the papers passing through the same as may be requisite to defray the expenses of the said office—appointing all officers of the land forces, in the service of the United States, excepting regimental officers—appointing all the officers of the naval forces, and commissioning all officers whatever in the service of the United States—making rules for the government and regulation of the said land and naval forces, and directing their operations.

The United States in Congress assembled shall have authority to appoint a committee, to sit in the recess of Congress, to be denominated 'A Committee of the States', and

These courts can't take territory away from individual states to give to the United States.

If asked, Congress will resolve private disputes involving land granted to settlers by two or more states in the same way Congress would resolve land disputes between two states.

Only Congress can determine the value of precious metals and money that the United States or individual states issue. Only Congress can set the standards of weights and measures throughout the country. Only Congress can regulate trade and manage relations with Native Americans who don't live in any of the states, as long as Congress doesn't violate the states' right to make their own laws. Only Congress can create and regulate interstate post offices and charge postage for interstate letters in order to maintain those post offices. Only Congress can appoint officers in the United States navies and armies, except for regimental officers. Only Congress can make rules to run and regulate the United States military and its operations.

Congress will have the power to create a committee called the "Committee of the States" that will meet whenever the full Congress is taking a break.

to consist of one delegate from each State; and to appoint such other committees and civil officers as may be necessary for managing the general affairs of the United States under their direction—to appoint one of their members to preside, provided that no person be allowed to serve in the office of president more than one year in any term of three years; to ascertain the necessary sums of money to be raised for the service of the United States, and to appropriate and apply the same for defraying the public expenses—to borrow money, or emit bills on the credit of the United States, transmitting every half-year to the respective States an account of the sums of money so borrowed or emitted—to build and equip a navy—to agree upon the number of land forces, and to make requisitions from each State for its quota, in proportion to the number of white inhabitants in such State; which requisition shall be binding, and thereupon the legislature of each State shall appoint the regimental officers, raise the men and cloath, arm and equip them in a solid-like manner, at the expense of the United States; and the officers and men so cloathed, armed and equipped shall march to the place appointed, and within the time agreed on by the United States in Congress assembled. But if the United States in Congress assembled shall, on consideration of circumstances judge proper that any State should not raise men, or should raise a smaller number of men than the quota thereof, such extra number shall be raised, officered, clothed, armed and equipped in the same manner as the quota of each State, unless the legislature of such State shall judge that such extra number cannot be safely spread out in the same, in which case they shall raise, officer, cloath, arm and equip as many of such extra number as they judge can be safely spared. And the officers and men so cloathed, armed, and equipped, shall march to the place appointed, and within the time agreed on by the United States in Congress assembled.

One Representative from each state will belong to this committee. Congress will also have the power to create committees and civilian positions that are necessary to manage the affairs of the United States. Congress will have the power to make one of its representatives the President, but this President can't serve more than one year during any three-year period. Congress will have the power to decide how much money should be collected to run the government and public expenses. Congress will have the power to borrow money or issue credit on behalf of the United States, but must inform the states of the amount to be borrowed every six months. Congress will have the power to build and maintain a navy, as well as to determine the size of the army. Congress will have the power to require each state to assign a number of troops to the United States land forces in proportion to the number of white residents in each state, and this requirement will be binding. Each state legislature will be required to appoint regimental officers, and recruit, arm, and equip soldiers with the proper munitions at the expense of the United States. The officers and other men appointed to the land forces must then march to a place Congress designates at a time Congress chooses. If a state doesn't raise the required number of men, then the extra men will still be chosen, equipped, and armed in a manner consistent with the original quota, unless the state legislature determines that to do so would threaten the safety of the state. In this case, the state legislature will recruit, arm, and equip as many men as possible. The officers and men will then march to the place and at the time Congress designates.

The United States in Congress assembled shall never engage in a war, nor grant letters of marque or reprisal in time of peace, nor enter into any treaties or alliances, nor coin money, nor regulate the value thereof, nor ascertain the sums and expenses necessary for the defense and welfare of the United States, or any of them, nor emit bills, nor borrow money on the credit of the United States, nor appropriate money, nor agree upon the number of vessels of war, to be built or purchased, or the number of land or sea forces to be raised, nor appoint a commander in chief of the army or navy, unless nine States assent to the same: nor shall a question on any other point, except for adjourning from day to day be determined, unless by the votes of the majority of the United States in Congress assembled.

The Congress of the United States shall have power to adjourn to any time within the year, and to any place within the United States, so that no period of adjournment be for a longer duration than the space of six months, and shall publish the journal of their proceedings monthly, except such parts thereof relating to treaties, alliances or military operations, as in their judgement require secrecy; and the yeas and nays of the delegates of each State on any question shall be entered on the journal, when it is desired by any delegates of a State, or any of them, at his or their request shall be furnished with a transcript of the said journal, except such parts as are above excepted, to lay before the legislatures of the several States.

ARTICLE X

The Committee of the States, or any nine of them, shall be authorized to execute, in the recess of Congress, such of the powers of Congress as the United States in Congress assembled, by the consent of the nine States, shall from time to time think expedient to vest them with; provided that no power be delegated to the said Committee, for the

Congress will never fight wars or grant letters of marque during peacetime. Congress will never make alliances; issue money or regulate its value; determine the cost of defending the United States or any one state; publish, borrow or print money; determine the number of warships to be built or purchased; determine the number of land and sea forces to be raised; or choose a commander-in-chief of the army or navy unless nine states agree. Congress will never make any other decisions, besides when to adjourn each day, without the agreement of nine states, unless a majority of Representatives in Congress agree.

Congress will have the power to take a break and meet another time later that year or in another place within the United States, but the break can't last longer than six months. Congress will publish a record of what the Representatives do each month, except for information about treaties, alliances, and military operations that they feel should be kept secret. The "yes" and "no" votes of the Representatives from each state will be recorded in the journal at the request of any representative. Except for the secretive portions mentioned above, the journal will be given to the state legislatures at the request of any Representative.

ARTICLE 10: THE COMMITTEE OF THE STATES

The Committee of the States, or any nine states, has the full authority of Congress when Congress is exercise of which, by the Articles of Confederation, the voice of nine States in the Congress of the United States assembled be requisite.

ARTICLE XI

Canada acceding to this confederation, and adjoining in the measures of the United States, shall be admitted into, and entitled to all the advantages of this Union; but no other colony shall be admitted into the same, unless such admission be agreed to by nine States.

ARTICLE XII

All bills of credit emitted, monies borrowed, and debts contracted by, or under the authority of Congress, before the assembling of the United States, in pursuance of the present confederation, shall be deemed and considered as a charge against the United States, for payment and satisfaction whereof the said United States, and the public faith are hereby solemnly pledged.

ARTICLE XIII

Every State shall abide by the determination of the United States in Congress assembled, on all questions which by this confederation are submitted to them. And the Articles of this Confederation shall be inviolably observed by every State, and the Union shall be perpetual; nor shall any alteration at any time hereafter be made in any of them; unless such alteration be agreed to in a Congress of the United States, and be afterwards confirmed by the legislatures of every State.

And Whereas it hath pleased the Great Governor of the World to incline the hearts of the legislatures we respectively represent in Congress, to approve of, and to authorize us to ratify the said Articles of Confederation and perpetual Union. Know Ye that we the undersigned delegates, by taking a break as long as the Committee doesn't grant itself powers without the approval of at least nine states.

ARTICLE 11: NEW TERRITORIES

Many early Americans hoped that Canadians would join in the revolution against Great Britain.

Canada will be admitted to the United States and entitled to the benefits of the confederacy if it agrees to the terms of these articles. No other colonies will be admitted, however, unless at least nine states agree.

ARTICLE 12: DEBTS

Congress will honor all of the debts previously acquired in accordance with these articles. The United States promises to satisfactorily pay these debts.

ARTICLE 13: PERMANENCE

Every state will obey the decisions on matters that are submitted to Congress. States must also obey the Articles of Confederation, and the union that they form will be permanent. The Articles of Confederation can't be changed unless Congress and all of the state legislatures agree.

The term ratify means to formally approve.

We hope that the Creator will convince the hearts of the men in the state legislatures to approve of the Articles of Confederation and authorize us to ratify them and create the permanent Union. Know that we virtue of the power and authority to us given for that purpose, do by these presents, in the name and in behalf of our respective constituents, fully and entirely ratify and confirm each and every of the said Articles of Confederation and perpetual Union, and all and singular the matters and things therein contained: And we do further solemnly plight and engage the faith of our respective constituents, that they shall abide by the determinations of the United States in Congress assembled, on all questions, which by the said Confederation are submitted to them. And that the Articles thereof shall be inviolably observed by the States we respectively represent, and that the Union shall be perpetual.

In Witness whereof we have hereunto set our hands in Congress. Done at Philadelphia in the State of Pennsylvania the ninth day of July in the year of our Lord One Thousand Seven Hundred and Seventy-Eight, and in the Third Year of the independence of America.

ON THE PART AND BEHALF OF THE STATE OF NEW HAMPSHIRE:
Josiah Bartlett; John Wentworth Junr. August 8th 1778

ON THE PART AND BEHALF OF THE STATE OF MASSACHUSETTS BAY:
John Hancock; Samuel Adams; Elbridge Gerry; Francis Dana; James Lovell; Samuel Holten

ON THE PART AND BEHALF OF THE STATE OF RHODE ISLAND AND PROVIDENCE PLANTATIONS:
William Ellery; Henry Marchant; John Collins

ON THE PART AND BEHALF OF THE STATE OF CONNECTICUT:
Roger Sherman; Samuel Huntington; Oliver Wolcott; Titus Hosmer; Andrew Adams

signers approve of every single one of these articles and of the permanent Union that will be created. We ask for the faith of the people we represent and ask that they'll obey Congress's decisions on all matters submitted by the states. We also ask that the states obey and respect the Articles of Confederation and that the Union be permanent.

We have come together in Philadelphia, Pennsylvania, on July 9, 1778, to form the Congress in the third year of the independence of the United States, as witnessed by:

NEW HAMPSHIRE, AUGUST 8, 1778
Josiah Bartlett; John Wentworth, Jr.

MASSACHUSETTS BAY
John Hancock; Samuel Adams; Elbridge Gerry; Francis Dana; James Lovell; Samuel Holten

RHODE ISLAND AND PROVIDENCE PLANTATIONS
William Ellery; Henry Marchant; John Collins

CONNECTICUT
Roger Sherman; Samuel Huntington; Oliver Wolcott; Titus Hosmer; Andrew Adams

ON THE PART AND BEHALF OF THE STATE OF NEW YORK:
James Duane; Francis Lewis; Wm Duer; Gouv Morris

ON THE PART AND IN BEHALF OF THE STATE OF NEW JERSEY, NOVEMBER 26, 1778:
Jno Witherspoon; Nath. Scudder

ON THE PART AND BEHALF OF THE STATE OF PENNSYLVANIA:
Robt Morris; Daniel Roberdeau; John Bayard Smith; William Clingan; Joseph Reed 22nd July 1778

ON THE PART AND BEHALF OF THE STATE OF DELAWARE:
Tho McKean February 12, 1779; John Dickinson May 5th 1779; Nicholas Van Dyke

ON THE PART AND BEHALF OF THE STATE OF MARYLAND:
John Hanson March 1 1781; Daniel Carroll Do

ON THE PART AND BEHALF OF THE STATE OF VIRGINIA:
Richard Henry Lee; John Banister; Thomas Adams; Jno Harvie; Francis Lightfoot Lee

ON THE PART AND BEHALF OF THE STATE OF NO CAROLINA:
John Penn July 21St 1778; Corns Harnett; Jno Williams

ON THE PART AND BEHALF OF THE STATE OF SOUTH CAROLINA:
Henry Laurens; William Henry Drayton; Jno Mathews; Richd Hutson; Thos Heyward Junr

ON THE PART AND BEHALF OF THE STATE OF GEORGIA:
Jno Walton 24th July 1778; Edwd Telfair; Edwd Langworthy

NEW YORK

James Duane; Francis Lewis; William Duer;
Gouverneur Morris

As you can see in the original text, it was
customary to abbreviate first names.
"Wm" was short for "William," "Tho"
was short for "Thomas," and "Jno" for
"John," etc.

NEW JERSEY, NOVEMBER 26, 1778

John Witherspoon; Nathaniel Scudder

PENNSYLVANIA, JULY 22, 1778

Robert Morris; Daniel Roberdeau; John Bayard
Smith; William Clingan; Joseph Reed

DELAWARE, 1779

Thomas McKean, February 12; John Dickinson,
May 5; Nicholas Van Dyke

MARYLAND, MARCH 1, 1781

John Hanson; Daniel Carroll

VIRGINIA

Richard Henry Lee; John Banister; Thomas Adams;
John Harvie; Francis Lightfoot Lee

NORTH CAROLINA, JULY 21, 1778

John Penn; Corns Harnett; John Williams

SOUTH CAROLINA

Henry Laurens; William Henry Drayton; John
Mathews; Richard Hutson; Thomas Heyward, Jr.

GEORGIA, JULY 24, 1778

John Walton; Edward Telfair; Edward Langworthy

THE
U.S. CONSTITUTION

Congress's inability to control the states prompted American leaders to meet in Philadelphia in 1787 to revise the Articles of Confederation. They quickly decided, however, to write an entirely new constitution to create a stronger and more stable national government. Even though all of the fifty-five delegates were wealthy landowners, they believed that they needed to create a government that would represent all classes of Americans.

The new Constitution created a government consisting of three branches: legislative (Congress), executive (the President), and judicial (headed by the Supreme Court). Delegates believed that this separation of powers would prevent the United States from becoming another monarchy.

Many delegates, however, feared that the separation of powers wasn't enough to prevent one branch of government from dominating the others, so they also created a system of checks and balances to distribute power even further. Checks and balances—such as the President's ability to veto legislation and the Supreme Court's ability to interpret the Constitution— gave each government branch the ability to monitor the others. The delegates also feared pure democracy because they didn't want a government controlled by commoners. They therefore made sure that the Constitution would only allow the "best men" to run the country.

When they had finished writing the Constitution, the delegates presented it to the states for ratification, or formal approval. They decided that nine of the thirteen states had to ratify the document in order for it to replace the Articles of Confederation.

Some people, called Federalists, favored the Constitution because it created a stronger, more stable government. Anti-Federalists, on the other hand, worried that the new government would have too much power over the states and the people. Some states ratified the Constitution immediately, but others did not.

To help convince Americans to ratify the Constitution, Alexander Hamilton, James Madison, and John Jay anonymously published a series of essays now known as *The Federalist Papers*. These essays discussed the benefits of a strong central government and assured readers that their rights wouldn't be taken away. James Madison also wrote a Bill of Rights, which outlined rights for both individuals and states. These rights eventually became the first ten amendments to the Constitution. By 1789, all thirteen states had ratified the Constitution.

OUTLINE

Preamble: Introduction to the Constitution

Article I: The Legislative Branch (Congress)
    Section 1: Overview of Congress
    Section 2: The House of Representatives
    Section 3: The Senate
    Section 4: Elections and Meetings
    Section 5: Procedural Rules
    Section 6: Salaries and Restrictions
    Section 7: How Congress Makes Laws
    Section 8: What Congress Can Do
    Section 9: What Congress Can't Do
    Section 10: What the States Can't Do

Article II: The Executive Branch (The Presidency)
    Section 1: Overview of the Presidency and Elections
    Section 2: What the President Can Do
    Section 3: The President's Duties
    Section 4: Removing the President from Office

Article III: The Judicial Branch (The Federal Courts)
    Section 1: Overview of the Federal Courts
    Section 2: What the Federal Courts Can Do
    Section 3: Treason

Article IV: The States and the People
    Section 1: Keeping State Records
    Section 2: Citizens' Basic Rights
    Section 3: New States and Territories
    Section 4: The Federal Government's Guarantee to
        the States

THE CONSTITUTION

PREAMBLE

We the People of the United States, in Order to form a more perfect Union, establish Justice, insure domestic Tranquility, provide for the common defence, promote the general Welfare, and secure the Blessings of Liberty to ourselves and our Posterity, do ordain and establish this Constitution for the United States of America.

ARTICLE I

SECTION 1

All legislative Powers herein granted shall be vested in a Congress of the United States, which shall consist of a Senate and House of Representatives.

SECTION 2

The House of Representatives shall be composed of Members chosen every second Year by the People of the several States, and the Electors in each State shall have the Qualifications requisite for Electors of the most numerous Branch of the State Legislature.

No Person shall be a Representative who shall not have attained to the Age of twenty five Years, and been seven Years a Citizen of the United States, and who shall not, when elected, be an Inhabitant of that State in which he shall be chosen.

THE CONSTITUTION

PREAMBLE: INTRODUCTION

We the people of the United States are writing this Constitution to create a better country, establish justice, ensure peace, defend the country, cultivate general happiness, and guarantee freedom for ourselves and future generations.

ARTICLE 1: THE LEGISLATIVE BRANCH (CONGRESS)

SECTION 1: OVERVIEW OF CONGRESS

Congress will make laws for the country. Congress will be divided into two houses, or parts: the Senate and the House of Representatives.

SECTION 2: THE HOUSE OF REPRESENTATIVES

The people of each state will elect members to the House of Representatives every two years. To elect members into the House of Representatives, voters must first be eligible to elect representatives to the largest house of their state legislatures.

Members of the House of Representatives must be at least twenty-five years old, U.S. citizens for at least seven years, and residents of the state they represent.

[Representatives and direct Taxes shall be apportioned among the several States which may be included within this Union, according to their respective Numbers, which shall be determined by adding to the whole Number of free Persons, including those bound to Service for a Term of Years, and excluding Indians not taxed, three fifths of all other Persons.][1] The actual Enumeration shall be made within three Years after the first Meeting of the Congress of the United States, and within every subsequent Term of ten Years, in such Manner as they shall by Law direct. The number of Representatives shall not exceed one for every thirty Thousand, but each State shall have at Least one Representative; and until such enumeration shall be made, the State of New Hampshire shall be entitled to chuse three, Massachusetts eight, Rhode Island and Providence Plantations one, Connecticut five, New York six, New Jersey four, Pennsylvania eight, Delaware one, Maryland six, Virginia ten, North Carolina five, South Carolina five, and Georgia three.

When vacancies happen in the Representation from any State, the Executive Authority thereof shall issue Writs of Election to fill such Vacancies.

The House of Representatives shall chuse their Speaker and other Officers; and shall have the sole Power of Impeachment.

SECTION 3

The Senate of the United States shall be composed of two Senators from each State, [chosen by the Legislature thereof,][2] for six Years; and each Senator shall have one Vote.

Indentured servants *agreed to serve a certain number of years under contract with the promise of receiving land upon regaining their freedom.*

This is the infamous three-fifths clause: each slave was counted as three-fifths of a person when calculating population. Native Americans were not counted at all.

Congress passed a law in 1929 that limited the number of members in the House of Representatives to 435. Otherwise, there'd be almost 10,000 Representatives today!

[The population of each state will determine the number of members it has in the House of Representatives and the amount it pays in direct taxes. A state's population will be determined by adding the number of free people, including indentured servants, and three-fifths of all other people, except for Native Americans who don't pay taxes.][1] The population will be counted three years after Congress first meets and then again every ten years after that in whatever way Congress decides. Each state gets one member in the House of Representatives for every 30,000 people, but every state gets at least one member even if it has fewer than 30,000 people. Until the population of each state is determined, New Hampshire gets three members in the House of Representatives, Massachusetts eight, Rhode Island one, Connecticut five, New York six, New Jersey four, Pennsylvania eight, Delaware one, Maryland six, Virginia ten, North Carolina five, South Carolina five, and Georgia three.

If a member of the House of Representatives dies or leaves office, the governor of that state will call for a special election to elect a new member.

The House of Representatives will pick its own leaders, including the Speaker of the House. Only the House of Representatives can impeach, or formally accuse, other government officials of committing crimes.

SECTION 3: THE SENATE

Each state will have two Senators serving in the Senate. [State legislatures choose their state's Senators,][2] who serve six-year terms and have one vote each.

---

1.   *Changed by the 14th Amendment.*
2.   *Changed by the 17th Amendment.*

Immediately after they shall be assembled in Consequence of the first Election, they shall be divided as equally as may be into three Classes. The Seats of the Senators of the first Class shall be vacated at the Expiration of the second Year, of the second Class at the Expiration of the fourth Year, and of the third Class at the Expiration of the sixth Year, so that one-third may be chosen every second Year; [and if Vacancies happen by Resignation, or otherwise, during the Recess of the Legislature of any State, the Executive thereof may make temporary Appointments until the next Meeting of the Legislature, which shall then fill such Vacancies.][3]

No person shall be a Senator who shall not have attained to the Age of thirty Years, and been nine Years a Citizen of the United States, and who shall not, when elected, be an Inhabitant of that State for which he shall be chosen.

The Vice President of the United States shall be President of the Senate, but shall have no Vote, unless they be equally divided.

The Senate shall chuse their other Officers, and also a President pro tempore, in the Absence of the Vice President, or when he shall exercise the Office of President of the United States.

The Senate shall have the sole Power to try all Impeachments. When sitting for that Purpose, they shall be on Oath or Affirmation. When the President of the United States is tried, the Chief Justice shall preside: And no Person shall be convicted without the Concurrence of two thirds of the Members present.

So that one-third of all the Senators are selected every two years, Senators will be divided into three groups roughly equal in size immediately after the first election. Senators in the first group will be reappointed or replaced after two years, Senators in the second group will be reappointed or replaced after four years, and Senators in the third group will be reappointed or replaced after six years. This way, one-third of all the Senators are selected every two years. [If a Senator dies or leaves during a time when state legislators are on a break, the governor or official in charge of that state may pick a new person to fill the Senate position until the state legislators meet again.][3]

Senators must be at least thirty years old, U.S. citizens for at least nine years, and residents of the state they represent.

The Vice President of the United States will also be the President of the Senate, but can vote only when there is a tie vote among the Senators.

The Senate will pick its own leaders, including the President Pro Tempore, who runs the Senate when the Vice President is away or if the Vice President becomes the President of the United States.

Only the Senate can try impeached officials accused of committing crimes. Senators must be under oath when trying an official. The Chief Justice of the Supreme Court will be in charge when the Senate is trying the President of the United States. The Senate can convict someone only with the agreement of two-thirds of the Senators.

---

3.   *Changed by the 17th Amendment.*

Judgment in Cases of Impeachment shall not extend further than to removal from Office, and disqualification to hold and enjoy any Office of honor, Trust or Profit under the United States: but the Party convicted shall nevertheless be liable and subject to Indictment, Trial, Judgment and Punishment, according to Law.

SECTION 4

The Times, Places and Manner of holding Elections for Senators and Representatives, shall be prescribed in each State by the Legislature thereof; but the Congress may at any time by Law make or alter such Regulations, except as to the Place of Chusing Senators.

The Congress shall assemble at least once in every Year, and such Meeting shall be on the [first Monday in December,][4] unless they shall by Law appoint a different Day.

SECTION 5

Each House shall be the Judge of the Elections, Returns and Qualifications of its own Members, and a Majority of each shall constitute a Quorum to do Business; but a smaller number may adjourn from day to day, and may be authorized to compel the Attendance of absent Members, in such Manner, and under such Penalties as each House may provide.

Each House may determine the Rules of its Proceedings, punish its Members for disorderly Behavior, and, with the Concurrence of two thirds, expel a Member.

Each House shall keep a Journal of its Proceedings, and from time to time publish the same, excepting such Parts as may in their Judgment require Secrecy; and the Yeas and Nays of the Members of either House on any question

The Senate can remove convicted people from their jobs but can't punish them in any other way. Convicted people cannot run for political office again or be appointed to any high offices, and they may still be tried and sentenced in a criminal court.

SECTION 4: ELECTIONS AND MEETINGS

State legislatures decide when, where, and how to hold elections for their states' Senators and Representatives. Congress can pass laws changing these regulations but can't determine where state legislators meet to choose Senators.

Congress must meet at least once a year, on the [first Monday in December,][4] unless Congress passes a law designating a different day.

SECTION 5: PROCEDURAL RULES

Each branch of Congress will decide on the elections and requirements for its members. To pass laws, a quorum, or majority of members, must be present, though other members can be absent from time to time. The House and Senate can require members to attend sessions and penalize absent members.

The House and Senate can make their own rules, punish their members for misbehavior, and expel a member if two-thirds agree.

The House and Senate records are collectively called The Congressional Record. The Senate and the House will both keep records of their activities and will publish these records from time to time, omitting the parts they want to keep confidential. How each House and Senate member voted

---

4.   *Changed by the 20th Amendment.*

shall, at the Desire of one fifth of those Present, be entered on the Journal.

Neither House, during the Session of Congress, shall, without the Consent of the other, adjourn for more than three days, nor to any other Place than that in which the two Houses shall be sitting.

SECTION 6

The Senators and Representatives shall receive a Compensation for their Services, to be ascertained by Law, and paid out of the Treasury of the United States. They shall in all Cases, except Treason, Felony and Breach of the Peace, be privileged from Arrest during their Attendance at the Session of their respective Houses, and in going to and returning from the same; and for any Speech or Debate in either House, they shall not be questioned in any other Place.

No Senator or Representative shall, during the Time for which he was elected, be appointed to any civil Office under the Authority of the United States, which shall have been created, or the Emoluments whereof shall have been encreased during such time; and no Person holding any Office under the United States, shall be a Member of either House during his Continuance in Office.

SECTION 7

All Bills for raising Revenue shall originate in the House of Representatives; but the Senate may propose or concur with Amendments as on other Bills.

Every Bill which shall have passed the House of Representatives and the Senate, shall, before it become a Law, be presented to the President of the United States; If he approve he shall sign it, but if not he shall return it, will be included on the published record if one-fifth of the members agree to do so.

The members of the House of Representatives and the Senate can't take a break longer than three days during a session of Congress without the agreement of the other house. The Senate and the House must meet in the same location.

SECTION 6: SALARIES AND RESTRICTIONS

Senators and Representatives will be paid a salary determined by law with money from the Treasury of the United States. They can't be arrested for crimes, except treason and felonies, while meeting in Congress or when traveling to meetings of Congress. They don't have to answer questions outside of Congress about anything they say while meeting in the House or the Senate.

Senators and Representatives can't be appointed to newly created civilian jobs or to jobs with higher salaries in the U.S. government while serving their term in Congress. Other U.S. government officials can't become a Senator or a Representative while serving in office.

SECTION 7: HOW CONGRESS MAKES LAWS

New bills, or laws, to raise taxes can be proposed only in the House of Representatives, but other bills can be proposed in the House or the Senate.

Bills go to the President of the United States after being passed in both the House of Representatives and the Senate. If the President approves, he will sign the bill and it will become a law. If he disapproves, he with his Objections to that House in which it shall have originated, who shall enter the Objections at large on their Journal, and proceed to reconsider it. If after such Reconsideration two thirds of that House shall agree to pass the Bill, it shall be sent, together with the Objections, to the other House, by which it shall likewise be reconsidered, and if approved by two thirds of that House, it shall become a Law. But in all such Cases the Votes of both Houses shall be determined by Yeas and Nays, and the Names of the Persons voting for and against the Bill shall be entered on the Journal of each House respectively. If any Bill shall not be returned by the President within ten Days (Sundays excepted) after it shall have been presented to him, the Same shall be a Law, in like Manner as if he had signed it, unless the Congress by their Adjournment prevent its Return, in which Case it shall not be a Law.

Every Order, Resolution, or Vote to which the Concurrence of the Senate and House of Representatives may be necessary (except on a question of Adjournment) shall be presented to the President of the United States; and before the Same shall take Effect, shall be approved by him, or being disapproved by him, shall be repassed by two thirds of the Senate and House of Representatives, according to the Rules and Limitations prescribed in the Case of a Bill.

SECTION 8

The Congress shall have Power To lay and collect Taxes, Duties, Imposts and Excises, to pay the Debts and provide for the common Defence and general Welfare of the United States; but all Duties, Imposts and Excises shall be uniform throughout the United States;

To borrow money on the credit of the United States;

will return the bill along with reasons why he dislikes it to the house that originally proposed the bill. The House or Senate will record and consider the President's objections. If, after review, two-thirds of the Senators and two-thirds of the Representatives again vote in favor of the bill, the bill will become a law in spite of the President's objections. The House and Senate will record the names and votes of their members in their own records. If the President doesn't sign or return a proposed bill to Congress within ten days (not including Sundays) after receiving it, then the bill automatically becomes a law. If Congress is on a break at that time, then the bill doesn't become a law.

The president's refusal to sign a bill ten days before Congress takes a break is known as a pocket veto.

The President must approve all votes and resolutions that both the Senate and House of Representatives pass (except for votes to take a break). If the President doesn't approve, two-thirds of the Senators and Representatives can vote to override the President's objection, just as they would to pass a bill the President disapproves.

SECTION 8: WHAT CONGRESS CAN DO

Congress can set and collect taxes to pay the national debt, build an army, and ensure the general well-being of the country. Taxes set by Congress must be the same throughout the country.

Congress can borrow money on behalf of the country.

To regulate Commerce with foreign Nations, and among the several States, and with the Indian Tribes;

To establish an uniform Rule of Naturalization, and uniform Laws on the subject of Bankruptcies throughout the United States;

To coin Money, regulate the Value thereof, and of foreign Coin, and fix the Standard of Weights and Measures;

To provide for the Punishment of counterfeiting the Securities and current Coin of the United States;

To establish Post Offices and post Roads;

To promote the Progress of Science and useful Arts, by securing for limited Times to Authors and Inventors the exclusive Right to their respective Writings and Discoveries;

To constitute Tribunals inferior to the supreme Court;

To define and punish Piracies and Felonies committed on the high Seas, and Offenses against the Law of Nations;

To declare War, grant Letters of Marque and Reprisal, and make Rules concerning Captures on Land and Water;

To raise and support Armies, but no Appropriation of Money to that Use shall be for a longer Term than two Years;

Congress can oversee business with other countries, between states, and with Native Americans.

Congress can establish rules for immigration and make laws regarding bankruptcy.

Congress can print money and establish its value relative to the money of other countries. Congress can also decide the value of weights and measures.

Congress can determine the punishment for people who print counterfeit money.

Congress can establish post offices and postal routes.

Congress can issue patents and copyrights for limited amounts of time to protect the inventions and writings of scientists and authors and to encourage the development of science and other skills that benefit society.

Congress can establish a system of legal courts below the Supreme Court.

Congress can determine what constitutes a crime at sea and decide how to punish the individuals or countries that commit these crimes.

Congress can declare war, allow private ships to capture enemy ships during war, and make rules about capturing enemies on land and at sea.

Congress can create and fund an army but can't give money to the army for more than a two-year period without reevaluation.

To provide and maintain a Navy;

To make Rules for the Government and Regulation of the land and naval Forces;

To provide for calling forth the Militia to execute the Laws of the Union, suppress Insurrections and repel Invasions;

To provide for organizing, arming, and disciplining the Militia, and for governing such Part of them as may be employed in the Service of the United States, reserving to the States respectively, the Appointment of the Officers, and the Authority of training the Militia according to the discipline prescribed by Congress;

To exercise exclusive Legislation in all Cases whatsoever, over such District (not exceeding ten Miles square) as may, by Cession of particular States, and the acceptance of Congress, become the Seat of the Government of the United States, and to exercise like Authority over all Places purchased by the Consent of the Legislature of the State in which the Same shall be, for the Erection of Forts, Magazines, Arsenals, dock-Yards, and other needful Buildings; —And

To make all Laws which shall be necessary and proper for carrying into Execution the foregoing Powers, and all other Powers vested by this Constitution in the Government of the United States, or in any Department or Officer thereof.

SECTION 9

The Migration or Importation of such Persons as any of the States now existing shall think proper to admit, shall not be prohibited by the Congress prior to the Year one thousand eight hundred and eight, but a tax or duty may be imposed on such Importation, not exceeding ten dollars for each Person.

Congress can create and fund a navy.

Congress can make rules to run and regulate the army and the navy.

A militia is an army made up of ordinary people, not professional soldiers.

Congress can order the civilian militias to enforce the laws of the country, end rebellions, and defend against invasions.

Congress can organize and provide weapons for the civilian militias. The states will appoint officers and train the militias according to the rules developed by Congress.

This separate district became the District of Columbia, or Washington, D.C.

This is the Necessary and Proper Clause that gives Congress the power to pass a variety of laws. It's often called the Elastic Clause *because it gives the government flexibility.*

Congress will have authority over the laws of the separate district that will become the official capital of the United States. This district will be no larger than ten square miles and will be given to Congress by the states. Congress will also have authority over land purchased from the states to build military bases and other government facilities.

Congress can make laws that are necessary and proper to do everything listed above and throughout this Constitution.

SECTION 9: WHAT CONGRESS CAN'T DO

Imported people were black slaves. The framers of the Constitution didn't use the term slave *in the Constitution to avoid the growing controversy over slavery.*

Congress can't stop the states from importing people until 1808, but it does have the right to tax states as much as ten dollars per imported person.

The privilege of the Writ of Habeas Corpus shall not be suspended, unless when in Cases of Rebellion or Invasion the public Safety may require it.

No Bill of Attainder or ex post facto Law shall be passed.

No capitation, or other direct, Tax shall be laid, [unless in Proportion to the Census or Enumeration herein before directed to be taken.][5]

No Tax or Duty shall be laid on Articles exported from any State.

No Preference shall be given by any Regulation of Commerce or Revenue to the Ports of one State over those of another: nor shall Vessels bound to, or from, one State, be obliged to enter, clear, or pay Duties in another.

No Money shall be drawn from the Treasury, but in Consequence of Appropriations made by Law; and a regular Statement and Account of the Receipts and Expenditures of all public Money shall be published from time to time.

No Title of Nobility shall be granted by the United States: And no Person holding any Office of Profit or Trust under them, shall, without the Consent of the Congress, accept of any present, Emolument, Office, or Title, of any kind whatever, from any King, Prince, or foreign State.

SECTION 10

No State shall enter into any Treaty, Alliance, or Confederation; grant Letters of Marque and Reprisal; coin Money; emit Bills of Credit; make any Thing but gold and silver

This is called the Writ of Habeas Corpus. →
Congress can't imprison people without accusing them of a crime, except when a rebellion or invasion threatens the public safety.

These are called Bills of Attainder and ex post facto *laws, respectively.* →
Congress can't pass laws that take away individuals' civil rights or private property without a trial. Congress also can't pass laws that punish people for acts they committed before those acts became illegal.

Congress can't tax individuals directly [unless it taxes every citizen counted in the census mentioned earlier.][5]

Congress can't tax anything that the states export.

Congress can't favor one state over another in business matters. Congress can't tax ships entering one state from another state.

Congress can't spend money from the Treasury unless permitted by law and must publish a record of its expenses from time to time.

The U.S. government can't give people titles of nobility. People working in public offices can't accept gifts, offices, or titles from other rulers or countries without the approval of Congress.

SECTION 10: WHAT THE STATES CAN'T DO

States can't make treaties or alliances with other countries. They can't print their own money, issue public

---

5.   *Changed by the 16th Amendment.*

Coin a Tender in Payment of Debts; pass any Bill of Attainder, ex post facto Law, or Law impairing the Obligation of Contracts, or grant any Title of Nobility.

No State shall, without the Consent of the Congress, lay any Imposts or Duties on Imports or Exports, except what may be absolutely necessary for executing its inspection Laws: and the net Produce of all Duties and Imposts, laid by any State on Imports or Exports, shall be for the Use of the Treasury of the United States; and all such Laws shall be subject to the Revision and Control of the Congress.

No State shall, without the Consent of Congress, lay any duty of Tonnage, keep Troops, or Ships of War in time of Peace, enter into any Agreement or Compact with another State, or with a foreign Power, or engage in War, unless actually invaded, or in such imminent Danger as will not admit of delay.

ARTICLE II

SECTION 1

The executive Power shall be vested in a President of the United States of America. He shall hold his Office during the Term of four Years, and, together with the Vice-President, chosen for the same Term, be elected, as follows:

Each State shall appoint, in such Manner as the Legislature thereof may direct, a Number of Electors, equal to the whole Number of Senators and Representatives to which the State may be entitled in the Congress: but no Senator or loans, or authorize anything besides gold and silver money as payment for debts. States also can't seize private property, pass ex post facto laws, alter private contracts, or award titles of nobility to individuals.

States can't tax imports and exports without the approval of Congress, unless it is absolutely necessary for inspection purposes. Any taxes collected on imports and exports must be given to the U.S. government. Congress can revise state laws concerning taxes on imports and exports.

States can't tax the cargo of ships without the approval of Congress. They can't maintain troops or warships in times of peace or make agreements with other states or countries. States can't fight wars without the approval of Congress, except in defense against an invasion or in extreme emergencies when there is no time to consult Congress.

ARTICLE 2: THE EXECUTIVE BRANCH (THE PRESIDENCY)

SECTION 1: OVERVIEW OF THE PRESIDENCY AND ELECTIONS

The President of the United States is in charge of the executive branch of government. The President and the Vice President will serve four-year terms and be elected in the following way:

States will appoint, in any way they like, a number of special electors equal to their number of Senators and representatives in Congress.

This group of special electors is called the Electoral College.

Representative, or Person holding an Office of Trust or Profit under the United States, shall be appointed an Elector.

[The Electors shall meet in their respective States, and vote by Ballot for two persons, of whom one at least shall not be an Inhabitant of the same State with themselves. And they shall make a List of all the Persons voted for, and of the Number of Votes for each; which List they shall sign and certify, and transmit sealed to the Seat of the Government of the United States, directed to the President of the Senate. The President of the Senate shall, in the Presence of the Senate and House of Representatives, open all the Certificates, and the Votes shall then be counted. The Person having the greatest Number of Votes shall be the President, if such Number be a Majority of the whole Number of Electors appointed; and if there be more than one who have such Majority, and have an equal Number of Votes, then the House of Representatives shall immediately chuse by Ballot one of them for President; and if no Person have a Majority, then from the five highest on the List the said House shall in like Manner chuse the President. But in choosing the President, the Votes shall be taken by States, the Representation from each State having one Vote; a quorum for this Purpose shall consist of a Member or Members from two thirds of the States, and a Majority of all the States shall be necessary to a Choice. In every Case, after the Choice of the President, the Person having the greatest Number of Votes of the Electors shall be the Vice President. But if there should remain two or more who have equal Votes, the Senate shall chuse from them by Ballot the Vice-President.][6]

The Congress may determine the Time of chusing the Electors, and the Day on which they shall give their Votes;

No Senator, Representative, or other elected U.S. government official can serve as an elector, however.

[Electors will meet in their respective states and vote by ballot for two people, at least one of whom doesn't live in their state. They will record the names of the people they voted for and count the number of votes each person receives. The electors will then sign the list, seal it, and send it to the President of the Senate in the nation's capital. The President of the Senate will then open the sealed lists and count the votes in front of the Senate and the House of Representatives. The person who receives the majority of votes of all the appointed electors will become President. If there is a tie, the House of Representatives will immediately vote by ballot to decide which of the tied candidates will be President. If no candidate has a majority, the House will vote for President from among the five candidates who received the most votes. When voting for President in the House of Representatives, each state gets one vote and at least one member from two-thirds of the states must be present. The candidate who receives the majority of the state votes becomes President. After the President is elected, the candidate with the second greatest number of electoral votes will be the Vice President. If there is a tie between two or more of the remaining candidates, the Senate will vote to decide which of the tied candidates will become the Vice President.][6]

Congress decides when states must choose the electors and the day when the electors give their votes to the President of the Senate.

---

6.   *Changed by the 12th Amendment.*

which Day shall be the same throughout the United States.

No person except a natural born Citizen, or a Citizen of the United States, at the time of the Adoption of this Constitution, shall be eligible to the Office of President; neither shall any Person be eligible to that Office who shall not have attained to the Age of thirty-five Years, and been fourteen Years a Resident within the United States.

[In Case of the Removal of the President from Office, or of his Death, Resignation, or Inability to discharge the Powers and Duties of the said Office, the same shall devolve on the Vice President, and the Congress may by Law provide for the Case of Removal, Death, Resignation or Inability, both of the President and Vice President, declaring what Officer shall then act as President, and such Officer shall act accordingly, until the Disability be removed, or a President shall be elected.][7]

The President shall, at stated Times, receive for his Services, a Compensation, which shall neither be encreased nor diminished during the Period for which he shall have been elected, and he shall not receive within that Period any other Emolument from the United States, or any of them.

Before he enter on the Execution of his Office, he shall take the following Oath or Affirmation: —"I do solemnly swear (or affirm) that I will faithfully execute the Office of President of the United States, and will to the best of my Ability, preserve, protect and defend the Constitution of the United States."

This day must be the same day for electors in every state.

Only citizens born in the United States or those who are U.S. citizens when this Constitution becomes law can be the President of the United States. The President must be at least thirty-five years old and have lived in the United States for at least fourteen years.

[If the President is removed from office, dies, quits, or is unable to fulfill his duties, the Vice President will serve as President. If both the President and the Vice President are removed from office, die, quit, or are unable to fulfill their duties, then Congress will select another government official to serve as President. This person will act as the President until the President or Vice President can perform his duties again or until a new President is elected.][7]

The President will be paid a salary at predetermined times that won't change during his term in office. He can't receive any additional income from the U.S. government or the states during his time in office.

The President must make the following oath before assuming office: "I do solemnly swear (or affirm) that I will faithfully execute the Office of the President of the United States, and will to the best of my Ability, preserve, protect and defend the Constitution of the United States."

---

7.   *Changed by the 25th Amendment.*

SECTION 2

The President shall be Commander in Chief of the Army and Navy of the United States, and of the Militia of the several States, when called into the actual Service of the United States; he may require the Opinion, in writing, of the principal Officer in each of the executive Departments, upon any subject relating to the Duties of their respective Offices, and he shall have Power to Grant Reprieves and Pardons for Offenses against the United States, except in Cases of Impeachment.

He shall have Power, by and with the Advice and Consent of the Senate, to make Treaties, provided two thirds of the Senators present concur; and he shall nominate, and by and with the Advice and Consent of the Senate, shall appoint Ambassadors, other public Ministers and Consuls, Judges of the supreme Court, and all other Officers of the United States, whose Appointments are not herein otherwise provided for, and which shall be established by Law: but the Congress may by Law vest the Appointment of such inferior Officers, as they think proper, in the President alone, in the Courts of Law, or in the Heads of Departments.

The President shall have Power to fill up all Vacancies that may happen during the Recess of the Senate, by granting Commissions which shall expire at the End of their next Session.

SECTION 3

He shall from time to time give to the Congress Information of the State of the Union, and recommend to their Consideration such Measures as he shall judge necessary and expedient; he may, on extraordinary Occasions, convene both Houses, or either of them, and in Case of Disagreement between them, with Respect to the Time of Adjournment, he may adjourn them to such Time as he shall think proper;

SECTION 2: WHAT THE PRESIDENT CAN DO

The President will be the commander in chief of the army and navy, as well as the state militias when they're working under the U.S. government. The President can ask for the written opinions of the executive branch division heads about anything to do with their departments. The President can pardon people committed of crimes against the country, except impeached government officials.

The President has the power to make treaties with other countries as long as two-thirds of the Senators present agree. The President can appoint judges, ambassadors, and other government officials with the approval of the Senate. Congress can decide which lesser appointments the President, courts, and heads of different departments should make.

While the Senate is on vacation, the President can temporarily fill vacancies until the end of the Senate's next meeting.

SECTION 3: THE PRESIDENT'S DUTIES

The President will occasionally speak to Congress about the state of the Union, explaining the issues and laws that he thinks are important. He can bring the House, the Senate, or both together under special circumstances. If the House and Senate can't agree on a time to adjourn, the President will decide when they'll adjourn.

he shall receive Ambassadors and other public Ministers; he shall take Care that the Laws be faithfully executed, and shall Commission all the Officers of the United States.

SECTION 4

The President, Vice President and all civil Officers of the United States, shall be removed from Office on Impeachment for, and Conviction of, Treason, Bribery, or other high Crimes and Misdemeanors.

ARTICLE III

SECTION 1

The judicial Power of the United States, shall be vested in one supreme Court, and in such inferior Courts as the Congress may from time to time ordain and establish. The Judges, both of the supreme and inferior Courts, shall hold their Offices during good Behaviour, and shall, at stated Times, receive for their Services a Compensation, which shall not be diminished during their Continuance in Office.

SECTION 2

The judicial Power shall extend to all Cases, in Law and Equity, arising under this Constitution, the Laws of the United States, and Treaties made, or which shall be made, under their Authority; —to all Cases affecting Ambassadors, other public Ministers and Consuls; —to all Cases of admiralty and maritime Jurisdiction; —to Controversies to which the United States shall be a Party; —to Controversies between two or more States; [between a State and Citizens of another State;—][8] between Citizens of different States;

The President will meet ambassadors and leaders from other countries, carry out the laws Congress makes, and appoint the officers of the U.S. government.

SECTION 4: REMOVING THE PRESIDENT FROM OFFICE

The President, Vice President, and other civilian officials in the U.S. government can be removed from their jobs if impeached for treason, bribery, and other crimes.

ARTICLE 3: THE JUDICIAL BRANCH (THE FEDERAL COURTS)

SECTION 1: OVERVIEW OF THE FEDERAL COURTS

The Constitution does not establish a federal court system but says Congress must create one. The Judiciary Act of 1789, one of the first acts Congress passed, created the federal courts. Congress named the head court the Supreme Court.

The judicial branch will consist of a head court and a system of lower courts that Congress creates from time to time. The judges presiding over these courts will keep their positions for life so long as they maintain good behavior. Judges will receive their salaries at predetermined times, which won't be reduced during their terms of service.

SECTION 2: WHAT THE FEDERAL COURTS CAN DO

The judicial branch will have authority over cases involving the laws of this Constitution, the laws of the United States, treaties, and cases concerning ambassadors and other foreign representatives. The federal courts will also have authority over cases related to shipping regulations and conflicts at sea, cases involving the U.S. government, and cases concerning disagreements between two or more state governments. [The judicial branch will also have jurisdiction in cases between a state government and a citizen from another state,][8] between citizens from different states,

---

8.   *Changed by the 11th Amendment.*

—between Citizens of the same State claiming Lands under Grants of different States, [and between a State, or the Citizens thereof, and foreign States, Citizens or Subjects.][9]

In all Cases affecting Ambassadors, other public Ministers and Consuls, and those in which a State shall be Party, the supreme Court shall have original Jurisdiction. In all the other Cases before mentioned, the supreme Court shall have appellate Jurisdiction, both as to Law and Fact, with such Exceptions, and under such Regulations as the Congress shall make.

The Trial of all Crimes, except in Cases of Impeachment, shall be by Jury; and such Trial shall be held in the State where the said Crimes shall have been committed; but when not committed within any State, the Trial shall be at such Place or Places as the Congress may by Law have directed.

SECTION 3

Treason against the United States, shall consist only in levying War against them, or in adhering to their Enemies, giving them Aid and Comfort. No Person shall be convicted of Treason unless on the Testimony of two Witnesses to the same overt Act, or on Confession in open Court.

The Congress shall have power to declare the Punishment of Treason, but no Attainder of Treason shall work Corruption of Blood, or Forfeiture except during the Life of the Person attainted.

between citizens of the same state fighting over land that other states gave to them, and [between a state government or its citizens and a foreign country or foreigners.]⁹

This is called original jurisdiction. ——→

The head court will hear only those cases involving ambassadors and other foreign representatives and cases directly involving a state government. Congress can make exceptions to this rule. The head court will hear only those cases mentioned above that other federal courts have already heard.

——→ *This is called appellate jurisdiction.*

Trials for any crime committed will be tried by a jury, except for impeachment trials. Trials will take place in the state where the crime occurred. Congress can decide where to hold the trial if the crime wasn't committed in any state.

SECTION 3: TREASON

Treason is defined as waging war against the United States or assisting its enemies. No one can be convicted of treason unless two witnesses testify or the suspect confesses in open court.

——→ *The English practice of punishing the family members of the accused was referred to as Corruption of Blood.*

Congress will decide the punishment for treason, but the punishment can't be extended to a traitor's relatives. Congress can confiscate a traitor's property only while he is still alive.

---

9.   *Changed by the 11th Amendment.*

ARTICLE IV

SECTION 1

Full Faith and Credit shall be given in each State to the public Acts, Records, and judicial Proceedings of every other State. And the Congress may by general Laws prescribe the Manner in which such Acts, Records and Proceedings shall be proved, and the Effect thereof.

SECTION 2

The Citizens of each State shall be entitled to all Privileges and Immunities of Citizens in the several States.

A Person charged in any State with Treason, Felony, or other Crime, who shall flee from Justice, and be found in another State, shall on demand of the executive Authority of the State from which he fled, be delivered up, to be removed to the State having Jurisdiction of the Crime.

[No Person held to Service or Labour in one State, under the Laws thereof, escaping into another, shall, in Consequence of any Law or Regulation therein, be discharged from such Service or Labour, but shall be delivered up on Claim of the Party to whom such Service or Labour may be due.][10]

SECTION 3

New States may be admitted by the Congress into this Union; but no new States shall be formed or erected within the Jurisdiction of any other State; nor any State be formed by the Junction of two or more States, or parts of States, without the Consent of the Legislatures of the States concerned as well as of the Congress.

ARTICLE 4:
THE STATES AND THE PEOPLE

SECTION 1: KEEPING STATE RECORDS

Each state must respect the laws, public records, and court proceedings of other states. Congress can determine how such state laws, records, and court proceedings are made official, distributed, and enforced.

SECTION 2: CITIZENS' BASIC RIGHTS

Citizens of one state have the same rights as citizens of every other state.

Fugitives charged with committing treason or serious crimes that run away to another state will be returned to the state that has jurisdiction over the crime at the request of the executive official of that state.

This has been called the Fugitive Slave clause. *The term* service of labor *usually refers to slavery but can also refer to indentured servitude.*

[According to the laws concerning labor, individuals held to service of labor in one state who run away to another state won't be freed from their service of labor. Upon request, these fugitives will be returned to the person or organization that owns their service contracts.][10]

SECTION 3: NEW STATES AND TERRITORIES

Congress can admit new states into the United States. New states can't be formed in the territory of an existing state, however, or by joining two or more states or parts of states without the agreement of Congress and the respective state legislatures.

---

10.   *Changed by the 13th Amendment.*

The Congress shall have Power to dispose of and make all needful Rules and Regulations respecting the Territory or other Property belonging to the United States; and nothing in this Constitution shall be so construed as to Prejudice any Claims of the United States, or of any particular State.

SECTION 4

The United States shall guarantee to every State in this Union a Republican Form of Government, and shall protect each of them against Invasion; and on Application of the Legislature, or of the Executive (when the Legislature cannot be convened) against domestic Violence.

ARTICLE V

The Congress, whenever two thirds of both Houses shall deem it necessary, shall propose Amendments to this Constitution, or, on the Application of the Legislatures of two thirds of the several States, shall call a Convention for proposing Amendments, which, in either Case, shall be valid to all Intents and Purposes, as part of this Constitution, when ratified by the Legislatures of three fourths of the several States, or by Conventions in three fourths thereof, as the one or the other Mode of Ratification may be proposed by the Congress; Provided that no Amendment which may be made prior to the Year One thousand eight hundred and eight shall in any Manner affect the first and fourth Clauses in the Ninth Section of the first Article; and that no State, without its Consent, shall be deprived of its equal Suffrage in the Senate.

Congress can create and change the rules and policies about land and property belonging to the U. S. government. Nothing in this Constitution should be interpreted to distort the claims of the United States government or of a particular state government.

SECTION 4: THE FEDERAL GOVERNMENT'S GUARANTEE TO THE STATES

The U.S. government promises that each state will have a republican form of government. The U.S. government will protect the states from invasion, as well as from domestic rebellion, at the request of a state legislature or state executive if the legislature can't meet.

Republics are governments in which power lies with the citizens, who elect officials to represent them and their interests.

ARTICLE 5:
CHANGING THE CONSTITUTION

Congress can call a convention to propose making changes to this Constitution at any time when two-thirds of both the Senate and the House of Representatives agree or when two-thirds of the state legislatures agree. Any ratified amendments will become legitimate parts of this Constitution, whether ratified by three-fourths of the state legislatures or by ratifying conventions in three-fourths of the states, whichever Congress proposes. Amendments ratified before 1808 can't change Article 1, Section 9, Paragraphs 1 and 4 of this Constitution. Amendments can't take away a state's equal representation in the Senate without the consent of that state.

To ratify means to formally approve.

ARTICLE VI

All Debts contracted and Engagements entered into, before the Adoption of this Constitution, shall be as valid against the United States under this Constitution, as under the Confederation.

This Constitution, and the Laws of the United States which shall be made in Pursuance thereof; and all Treaties made, or which shall be made, under the Authority of the United States, shall be the supreme Law of the Land; and the Judges in every State shall be bound thereby, any Thing in the Constitution or Laws of any State to the Contrary notwithstanding.

The Senators and Representatives before mentioned, and the Members of the several State Legislatures, and all executive and judicial Officers, both of the United States and of the several States, shall be bound by Oath or Affirmation, to support this Constitution; but no religious Test shall ever be required as a Qualification to any Office or public Trust under the United States.

ARTICLE VII

The Ratification of the Conventions of nine States, shall be sufficient for the Establishment of this Constitution between the States so ratifying the Same.

Done in Convention by the Unanimous Consent of the States present the Seventeenth Day of September in the Year of our Lord one thousand seven hundred and Eighty seven and of the Independence of the United States of America the Twelfth. In Witness whereof We have hereunto subscribed our Names.

ARTICLE 6: THE AUTHORITY OF THE CONSTITUTION

The U.S. government will assume all the debts and obligations made prior to the ratification of this Constitution by the government operating under the Articles of Confederation.

The Constitution, and all laws and treaties made in accordance with it, will be the supreme law of the land—the highest law of the United States. Judges in every state must respect everything in the Constitution and disregard state laws that contradict it.

All Senators, Representatives, state legislators, and officials in the executive and judicial branches of the U.S. government and individual state governments must take an oath to uphold this Constitution. A religious test will never be required to hold any office or official position in the United States.

ARTICLE 7: RATIFYING THE CONSTITUTION

Once the Constitution is ratified by conventions in at least nine states, it will immediately take effect for those states.

This Constitution was completed with the unanimous agreement of all states present on September 17, 1787, during the twelfth year of American independence. We have signed our names below as witnesses.

Go. Washington—President and deputy from Virginia

NEW HAMPSHIRE:
John Langdon; Nicholas Gilman

MASSACHUSETTS:
Nathaniel Gorham; Rufus King

CONNECTICUT:
Wm. Saml. Johnson; Roger Sherman

NEW YORK:
Alexander Hamilton

NEW JERSEY:
Wil: Livingston; David Brearley; Wm. Paterson;
Jona: Dayton

PENSYLVANIA:
B Franklin; Thomas Mifflin; Robt Morris; Geo. Clymer;
Thos. Fitz Simons; Jared Ingersoll; James Wilson;
Gouv Morris

DELAWARE:
Geo: Read; Gunning Bedford jun; John Dickinson;
Richard Bassett; Jaco: Broom

MARYLAND:
James McHenry; Dan of St. Thos. Jenifer; Danl Carroll

VIRGINIA:
John Blair; James Madison jr

NORTH CAROLINA:
Wm. Blount; Richd. Dobbs Spaight; Hu Williamson

SOUTH CAROLINA:
J. Rutledge; Charles Cotesworth Pinckney; Charles
Pinckney; Pierce Butler

GEORGIA:
William Few; Abr Baldwin

Attest William Jackson, Secretary

Washington was president of the group of men who wrote the Constitution. He wasn't U.S. president when this document was written because that office didn't yet exist.

George Washington
President and representative from Virginia

NEW HAMPSHIRE
John Langdon; Nicholas Gilman

MASSACHUSETTS
Nathaniel Gorham; Rufus King

CONNECTICUT
William Samuel Johnson; Roger Sherman

NEW YORK
Alexander Hamilton

NEW JERSEY
William Livingston; David Brearley; William
Paterson; Jonathan Dayton

PENNSYLVANIA
Benjamin Franklin; Thomas Mifflin; Robert Morris;
George Clymer; Thomas FitzSimons; Jared Ingersoll;
James Wilson; Gouverneur Morris

DELAWARE
George Read; Gunning Bedford, Jr.; John Dickinson;
Richard Bassett; Jacob Broom

MARYLAND
James McHenry; Dan of St. Thomas Jenifer; Daniel
Carroll

VIRGINIA
John Blair; James Madison, Jr.

NORTH CAROLINA
William Blount; Richard Dobbs Spaight; Hugh
Williamson

SOUTH CAROLINA
John Rutledge; Charles Cotesworth Pinckney;
Charles Pinckney; Pierce Butler

GEORGIA
William Few; Abraham Baldwin

Certified by William Jackson, Secretary

Amendments

Congress shall make no law respecting an establishment of religion, or prohibiting the free exercise thereof; or abridging the freedom of speech, or of the press; or the right of the people peaceably to assemble, and to petition the Government for a redress of grievances.

AMENDMENT II

A well regulated Militia being necessary to the security of a free State, the right of the people to keep and bear Arms, shall not be infringed.

AMENDMENT III

No Soldier shall, in time of peace be quartered in any house, without the consent of the Owner, nor in time of war, but in a manner to be prescribed by law.

AMENDMENT IV

The right of the people to be secure in their persons, houses, papers, and effects, against unreasonable searches and seizures, shall not be violated, and no Warrants shall issue, but upon probable cause, supported by Oath or affirmation, and particularly describing the place to be searched, and the persons or things to be seized.

Amendments to the Constitution

THE BILL OF RIGHTS (1–10)

An amendment is an alteration or addition to the Constitution.

AMENDMENT 1. FREEDOM OF RELIGION, SPEECH, PRESS, ASSEMBLY, AND PETITION (1791)

Congress won't force religion on anyone or prevent people from practicing their religions. Congress won't interfere with people's freedom to speak and publish ideas or prevent people from meeting peacefully or complaining to the government when they're unhappy.

AMENDMENT 2. THE RIGHT TO BEAR ARMS (1791)

The courts have always believed this amendment upholds states' right to arm militias. Many conservatives, however, believe it upholds individuals' right to own guns.

The people have the right to have weapons because a strong militia is needed to protect a free country.

AMENDMENT 3. HOUSING SOLDIERS (1791)

Soldiers can't be housed in people's houses during peacetime or war without their permission. Congress will determine where soldiers will be housed.

AMENDMENT 4. PROTECTION AGAINST ILLEGAL SEARCH AND SEIZURE (1791)

A warrant is a court order authorizing police to arrest a person, search his or her private property, or take his or her belongings.

People, as well as their homes, papers, and possessions, can't be searched or taken without a good reason. Warrants can only be issued when there are grounds for suspicion, and they must describe the places to be searched and the people and objects to be taken.

AMENDMENT V

No person shall be held to answer for a capital, or otherwise infamous crime, unless on a presentment or indictment of a Grand Jury, except in cases arising in the land or naval forces, or in the Militia, when in actual service in time of War or public danger; nor shall any person be subject for the same offence to be twice put in jeopardy of life or limb; nor shall be compelled in any criminal case to be a witness against himself, nor be deprived of life, liberty, or property, without due process of law; nor shall private property be taken for public use, without just compensation.

AMENDMENT VI

In all criminal prosecutions, the accused shall enjoy the right to a speedy and public trial, by an impartial jury of the State and district wherein the crime shall have been committed, which district shall have been previously ascertained by law, and to be informed of the nature and cause of the accusation; to be confronted with the witnesses against him; to have compulsory process for obtaining witnesses in his favor, and to have the Assistance of Counsel for his defence.

AMENDMENT VII

In suits at common law, where the value in controversy shall exceed twenty dollars, the right of trial by jury shall be preserved, and no fact tried by a jury, shall be otherwise reexamined in any Court of the United States, than according to the rules of the common law.

AMENDMENT VIII

Excessive bail shall not be required, nor excessive fines imposed, nor cruel and unusual punishments inflicted.

AMENDMENT 5. TRIAL BY JURY AND PROTECTION OF PRIVATE PROPERTY (1791)

A grand jury is a jury of 12 to 23 people that examines evidence and decides whether the accused has committed a crime and if there should be a criminal trial.

Individuals can't be arrested for serious crimes until they have been formally accused by a grand jury, unless the individual is in the military or militia during wartime or in an emergency. Individuals can't be tried for the same crime twice. An individual doesn't have to say anything in court that will make him look guilty, and can't have his life, freedom, or property taken away illegally. Private property can't be taken for public use without fair compensation.

AMENDMENT 6. THE RIGHTS OF THE ACCUSED (1791)

The Supreme Court has never actually defined the length of a speedy trial, but judges decide depending on the circumstances. The government, however, can't keep an accused person in jail for a long time without trying him.

An individual accused of committing a crime will have the right to a speedy, public trial by an unbiased jury in the state and district in which the crime occurred. The accused has the right to know the charge against him and why he's being charged. He has the right to listen to witnesses testify again him and to call witnesses in his defense. He also has the right to a defense attorney.

AMENDMENT 7. TRIAL BY JURY IN CIVIL CASES (1791)

Juries will try all civil cases in which the disputed value is greater than twenty dollars. Other American courts can't overturn a jury's decision, unless the law has been applied incorrectly.

AMENDMENT 8. RESTRICTIONS ON PUNISHMENT (1791)

Most historians believe that cruel and unusual punishment meant torture and excessive prison terms, and the Supreme Court has ruled with this loose definition in mind.

Individuals shouldn't have to pay unreasonable bail or fines or suffer cruel and unusual punishment.

AMENDMENT IX

The enumeration in the Constitution, of certain rights, shall not be construed to deny or disparage others retained by the people.

AMENDMENT X

The powers not delegated to the United States by the Constitution, nor prohibited by it to the States, are reserved to the States respectively, or to the people.

AMENDMENT XI

The Judicial power of the United States shall not be construed to extend to any suit in law or equity, commenced or prosecuted against one of the United States by Citizens of another State, or by Citizens or Subjects of any Foreign State.

AMENDMENT XII

The Electors shall meet in their respective states and vote by ballot for President and Vice-President, one of whom, at least, shall not be an inhabitant of the same state with themselves; they shall name in their ballots the person voted for as President, and in distinct ballots the person voted for as Vice-President, and they shall make distinct lists of all persons voted for as President, and of all persons voted for as Vice-President, and of the number of votes for each, which lists they shall sign and certify, and transmit sealed to the seat of the government of the United States, directed to the President of the Senate;— The President of the Senate shall, in the presence of the Senate and House of Representatives, open all the certificates and the votes shall then be counted;—The person having the greatest number of votes for President, shall be the President, if such number be a majority of the whole number of Electors appointed; and if no person have such majority, then from the persons having the highest numbers not exceeding three on the list of those voted for as President, the House of Representatives shall choose immediately, by ballot, the President.

AMENDMENT 9. POWERS LEFT TO THE PEOPLE (1791)

Just because this Constitution specifies many rights doesn't mean that these are the only rights the people have.

AMENDMENT 10. POWERS LEFT TO THE STATES (1791)

The powers not mentioned in this Constitution that aren't given to the federal government and aren't forbidden to the states are left to the states and the people.

AMENDMENT 11. A RESTRICTION ON THE FEDERAL COURTS (1798)

Federal courts have no authority in lawsuits between a state government and citizens of another state or foreign country.

AMENDMENT 12. THE ELECTION OF PRESIDENTS AND VICE PRESIDENTS (1804)

Rivals Thomas Jefferson and Aaron Burr received the same number of electoral votes in the election of 1800, and the House of Representatives had to choose which man would be president and which would be vice president. The 12th Amendment was ratified soon after to change how presidents and vice presidents are elected to prevent this from happening again.

Electors will meet in their respective states and cast separate ballots for President and Vice President, at least one of whom doesn't live in their state. They will record the names of all individuals receiving votes for President on one list and the names of all individuals receiving votes for Vice President on a separate list. On each list, they will record the number of votes each person received. They will then sign the list, seal it, and send it to the President of the Senate in the nation's capital. The President of the Senate will then unseal the lists and count the votes in front of the Senate and the House of Representatives. The person who receives the majority of votes for President of all the appointed electors will become President. If no candidate has a majority, the House of Representatives will elect the President from the three candidates who received the most votes.

But in choosing the President, the votes shall be taken by states, the representation from each state having one vote; a quorum for this purpose shall consist of a member or members from two-thirds of the states, and a majority of all the states shall be necessary to a choice. [And if the House of Representatives shall not choose a President whenever the right of choice shall devolve upon them, before the fourth day of March next following, then the Vice-President shall act as President, as in the case of the death or other constitutional disability of the President—][11] The person having the greatest number of votes as Vice-President, shall be the Vice-President, if such number be a majority of the whole number of Electors appointed, and if no person have a majority, then from the two highest numbers on the list, the Senate shall choose the Vice-President; a quorum for the purpose shall consist of two-thirds of the whole number of Senators, and a majority of the whole number shall be necessary to a choice. But no person constitutionally ineligible to the office of President shall be eligible to that of Vice-President of the United States.

AMENDMENT XIII

SECTION 1. Neither slavery nor involuntary servitude, except as a punishment for crime whereof the party shall have been duly convicted, shall exist within the United States, or any place subject to their jurisdiction.

SECTION 2. Congress shall have power to enforce this article by appropriate legislation.

When voting for President in the House of Representatives, each state gets one vote. To take this vote, at
least one member from two-thirds of the states must
be present. The candidate who receives the majority
of the state votes becomes President. [If the House of
Representatives doesn't elect a President before
March 4th, then the Vice President will serve as the
President, just as he would if the President dies,
resigns, or leaves office.][11] The person who receives
the majority of votes for Vice President of all the
appointed electors will become the Vice President. If
no candidate receives a majority, the Senate will elect
the Vice President from the two candidates who
received the most votes. When voting for Vice President in the Senate, two-thirds of the Senators must be
present, and a majority vote of the total number of
Senators is required. People who aren't eligible to
become President can't become Vice President either.

THE CIVIL WAR (OR RECONSTRUCTION) AMENDMENTS (13–15)

AMENDMENT 13. SLAVERY OUTLAWED (1865)
SECTION 1. Slavery and forced labor are abolished in
the United States and its territories, except as a punishment for crimes.

SECTION 2. Congress can make laws to enforce this
amendment.

---

11.   *Changed by the 20th Amendment.*

AMENDMENT XIV

SECTION 1. All persons born or naturalized in the United States, and subject to the jurisdiction thereof, are citizens of the United States and of the State wherein they reside. No State shall make or enforce any law which shall abridge the privileges or immunities of citizens of the United States; nor shall any State deprive any person of life, liberty, or property, without due process of law; nor deny to any person within its jurisdiction the equal protection of the laws.

SECTION 2. Representatives shall be apportioned among the several States according to their respective numbers, counting the whole number of persons in each State, excluding Indians not taxed. But when the right to vote at any election for the choice of electors for President and Vice President of the United States, Representatives in Congress, the Executive and Judicial officers of a State, or the members of the Legislature thereof, is denied to any of the male inhabitants of such State, being twenty-one years of age, and citizens of the United States, or in any way abridged, except for participation in rebellion, or other crime, the basis of representation therein shall be reduced in the proportion which the number of such male citizens shall bear to the whole number of male citizens twenty-one years of age in such State.

SECTION 3. No person shall be a Senator or Representative in Congress, or elector of President and Vice President, or hold any office, civil or military, under the United States, or under any State, who, having previously taken an oath, as a member of Congress, or as an officer of the United States, or as a member of any State legislature, or as an executive or judicial officer of any State, to support the Constitution of the United States, shall have engaged in Insurrection or rebellion against the same, or given aid or comfort to the

AMENDMENT 14. AMERICAN CITIZENSHIP DEFINED (1868)

SECTION 1. Individuals who are born in the United States or who become U.S. citizens by choice are citizens of the United States and of the state in which they live. States can't make laws that alter or take away the privileges and rights of American citizenship. States can't take away an individual's life, freedom, or property illegally, and must protect their citizens equally under the law.

SECTION 2. The population of a state will determine the number of members it has in the House of Representatives. A state's population will be determined by adding the number of free people, except for Native Americans who don't pay taxes. Representation in the House of Representatives will be reduced if any male citizens over the age of twenty-one, who did not participate in a rebellion or other crime, are denied their right to vote for electors for President and Vice President, members of the House of Representatives, governors, state judges, and state legislators. Representation in the House will be reduced in proportion to the number of these excluded male voters.

SECTION 3. Individuals who participated in a rebellion against the United States or helped enemies of the United States after taking an oath to uphold the Constitution as a Congressman, federal official, state legislator, governor, or other official in any state can never become a Senator, Representative, Presidential or Vice Presidential elector, or serve as a civil or military official in the federal government or state governments.

enemies thereof. But Congress may by a vote of two-thirds of each House, remove such disability.

SECTION 4. The validity of the public debt of the United States, authorized by law, including debts incurred for payment of pensions and bounties for services in suppressing insurrection or rebellion, shall not be questioned. But neither the United States nor any State shall assume or pay any debt or obligation incurred in aid of insurrection or rebellion against the United States, or any claim for the loss or emancipation of any slave; but all such debts, obligations and claims shall be held illegal and void.

SECTION 5. The Congress shall have power to enforce, by appropriate legislation, the provisions of this article.

AMENDMENT XV
SECTION 1. The right of citizens of the United States to vote shall not be denied or abridged by the United States or by any State on account of race, color, or previous condition of servitude.

SECTION 2. The Congress shall have power to enforce this article by appropriate legislation.

AMENDMENT XVI
The Congress shall have power to lay and collect taxes on incomes, from whatever source derived, without apportionment among the several States, and without regard to any census or enumeration.

Congress can lift this ban if two-thirds of the Senate and House of Representatives agree.

SECTION 4. The public debt of the United States, including debts acquired while suppressing insurrections and rebellions, are valid debts. But the United States and the individual states won't pay any debts acquired in support of a rebellion against the United States. Likewise, the United States won't compensate for lost or freed slaves. These debts are illegal and no longer valid.

SECTION 5. Congress can make laws to enforce this amendment.

AMENDMENT 15. VOTING RIGHTS FOR ALL CITIZENS (1870)

This amendment only applied to male voters. Women couldn't vote until 1920.

SECTION 1. The United States and individual states can't take away or hinder the right of citizens to vote because of their race or color or because they used to be slaves.

SECTION 2. Congress can make laws to enforce this amendment.

THE PROGRESSIVE AMENDMENTS (16–19)

AMENDMENT 16. THE FEDERAL INCOME TAX (1913)

Congress can establish and collect taxes on the money individuals make, however they make it, without regard to the population of the individual states.

AMENDMENT XVII

The Senate of the United States shall be composed of two Senators from each State, elected by the people thereof, for six years; and each Senator shall have one vote. The electors in each State shall have the qualifications requisite for electors of the most numerous branch of the State legislatures.

When vacancies happen in the representation of any State in the Senate, the executive authority of such State shall issue writs of election to fill such vacancies: *Provided*, That the legislature of any State may empower the executive thereof to make temporary appointments until the people fill the vacancies by election as the legislature may direct.

This amendment shall not be so construed as to affect the election or term of any Senator chosen before it becomes valid as part of the Constitution.

AMENDMENT XVIII

SECTION 1. [After one year from the ratification of this article the manufacture, sale, or transportation of intoxicating liquors within, the importation thereof into, or the exportation thereof from the United States and all territory subject to the jurisdiction thereof for beverage purposes is hereby prohibited.

SECTION 2. The Congress and the several States shall have concurrent power to enforce this article by appropriate legislation.

SECTION 3. This article shall be inoperative unless it shall have been ratified as an amendment to the Constitution by the legislatures of the several States, as provided in the Constitution, within seven years from the date of the submission hereof to the States by the Congress.]

AMENDMENT 17. THE DIRECT ELECTION OF SENATORS (1913)

Each state will have two Senators serving in the Senate. The people in each state will elect their Senators, who will serve six-year terms and have one vote each. To elect Senators, voters must first be eligible to elect representatives to the largest house of their state legislatures.

If a Senator dies or leaves office, the Governor of that state will call for a special election to elect a new Senator. In the meantime, the state legislature can allow the Governor to appoint someone to fill the empty Senate seat until the people elect a new Senator.

This amendment shouldn't be used to change the election or terms of Senators who were selected before this amendment takes effect.

AMENDMENT 18. PROHIBITION (1919)

SECTION 1. [Making, selling, and transporting alcohol within the United States, as well as importing and exporting alcohol to and from the United States and its territories, will be forbidden beginning one year after the ratification of this amendment.

SECTION 2. Congress and the states can both make laws to enforce this amendment.

SECTION 3. State legislatures must ratify this amendment, as outlined in the Constitution, within seven years after receiving it from Congress in order for it to be valid.][12]

---

12. *Repealed by the 21st Amendment.*

AMENDMENT XIX

The right of citizens of the United States to vote shall not be denied or abridged by the United States or by any State on account of sex.

Congress shall have power to enforce this article by appropriate legislation.

AMENDMENT XX

SECTION 1. The terms of the President and Vice President shall end at noon on the 20th day of January, and the terms of Senators and Representatives at noon on the 3d day of January, of the years in which such terms would have ended if this article had not been ratified; and the terms of their successors shall then begin.

SECTION 2. The Congress shall assemble at least once in every year, and such meeting shall begin at noon on the 3d day of January, unless they shall by law appoint a different day.

SECTION 3. If, at the time fixed for the beginning of the term of the President, the President elect shall have died, the Vice President elect shall become President. If a President shall not have been chosen before the time fixed for the beginning of his term, or if the President elect shall have failed to qualify, then the Vice President elect shall act as President until a President shall have qualified; and the Congress may by law provide for the case wherein neither a President elect nor a Vice President elect shall have qualified, declaring who shall then act as President, or the manner in which one who is to act shall be selected, and such person shall act accordingly until a President or Vice President shall have qualified.

The United States and individual states can't take away or hinder the right of citizens to vote because of their gender.

Congress can make laws to enforce this amendment.

FURTHER AMENDMENTS

AMENDMENT 20. PRESIDENTIAL AND CONGRESSIONAL TERMS (1933)
SECTION 1. Presidential and Vice Presidential terms will end at noon on January 20th. Senators' and Representatives' terms will end at noon on January 3rd during the year when their terms would have ended had this amendment not been ratified. Their successors' terms will then begin immediately.

SECTION 2. Congress must meet at least once a year, at noon on January 3rd, unless Congress passes a law designating a different day.

SECTION 3. The Vice President-elect will become President if the President-elect dies before his term begins. If a President hasn't been chosen by the start of his term or if the President-elect doesn't meet the qualifications of the Presidency, then the Vice President-elect will serve as President until an eligible President is chosen. If both the President-elect and the Vice President-elect aren't qualified, Congress can pass a law designating an Acting President or a law explaining what an Acting President should do until a President or Vice President is chosen.

SECTION 4. The Congress may by law provide for the case of the death of any of the persons from whom the House of Representatives may choose a President whenever the right of choice shall have devolved upon them, and for the case of the death of any of the persons from whom the Senate may choose a Vice President whenever the right of choice shall have devolved upon them.

SECTION 5. Sections 1 and 2 shall take effect on the 15th day of October following the ratification of this article.

SECTION 6. This article shall be inoperative unless it shall have been ratified as an amendment to the Constitution by the legislatures of three-fourths of the several States within seven years from the date of its submission.

AMENDMENT XXI

SECTION 1. The eighteenth article of amendment to the Constitution of the United States is hereby repealed.

SECTION 2. The transportation or importation into any State, Territory, or possession of the United States for delivery or use therein of intoxicating liquors, in violation of the laws thereof, is hereby prohibited.

SECTION 3. This article shall be inoperative unless it shall have been ratified as an amendment to the Constitution by conventions in the several States, as provided in the Constitution, within seven years from the date of the submission hereof to the States by the Congress.

AMENDMENT XXII

SECTION 1. No person shall be elected to the office of the President more than twice, and no person who has held the office of President, or acted as President, for more than two

SECTION 4. Congress can make laws explaining what to do after the death of a President who'd been appointed by the House of Representatives. Likewise, Congress can make laws explaining what to do if a Senate-appointed Vice President dies.

SECTION 5. Sections 1 and 2 of this amendment will take effect on October 15th after this amendment is ratified.

SECTION 6. Three-quarters of the state legislatures must ratify this amendment within seven years after receiving it from Congress in order for it to be valid.

AMENDMENT 21. PROHIBITION REPEALED (1933)

SECTION 1. The 18th Amendment to the Constitution is repealed.

The term repeal means to cancel.

SECTION 2. It is forbidden to transport and import alcohol in any state or territory of the United States where importing and transporting alcohol is illegal.

SECTION 3. State ratifying conventions must ratify this amendment, as outlined in the Constitution, within seven years of receiving it from Congress in order for it to be valid.

AMENDMENT 22. TWO-TERM LIMITATION FOR PRESIDENTS (1951)

SECTION 1. An individual can be elected to the Presidency only twice, and anyone who has served as President for more than two years during someone else's

years of a term to which some other person was elected President shall be elected to the office of the President more than once. But this Article shall not apply to any person holding the office of President when this Article was proposed by the Congress, and shall not prevent any person who may be holding the office of President, or acting as President, during the term within which this Article becomes operative from holding the office of President or acting as President during the remainder of such term.

SECTION 2. This article shall be inoperative unless it shall have been ratified as an amendment to the Constitution by the legislatures of three-fourths of the several States within seven years from the date of its submission to the States by the Congress.

AMENDMENT XXIII

SECTION 1. The District constituting the seat of Government of the United States shall appoint in such manner as the Congress may direct:

A number of electors of President and Vice President equal to the whole number of Senators and Representatives in Congress to which the District would be entitled if it were a State, but in no event more than the least populous State; they shall be in addition to those appointed by the States, but they shall be considered, for the purposes of the election of President and Vice President, to be electors appointed by a State; and they shall meet in the District and perform such duties as provided by the twelfth article of amendment.

SECTION 2. The Congress shall have power to enforce this article by appropriate legislation.

term can only be elected to the Presidency once. This amendment doesn't apply to individuals serving as President when this amendment was proposed or to individuals serving as President when this amendment takes effect.

SECTION 2. Three-quarters of the state legislatures must ratify this amendment within seven years after receiving it from Congress in order for it to be valid.

AMENDMENT 23. VOTING RIGHTS FOR RESIDENTS OF WASHINGTON, D.C. (1961)

SECTION 1. As directed by Congress, the district that serves as the nation's capital will appoint:

The same number of electors for the President and Vice President as the number of Senators and Representatives the district would have in Congress if it were a state. But the district will never have more electors than the least populous state. These electors will be added to the total number of electors appointed by other states and will be considered equal to electors appointed by states to elect Presidents and Vice Presidents. The electors of this district will meet in the district and perform their duties as outlined in the 12th Amendment.

SECTION 2. Congress can make laws to enforce this amendment.

AMENDMENT XXIV

SECTION 1. The right of citizens of the United States to vote in any primary or other election for President or Vice President, for electors for President or Vice President, or for Senator or Representative in Congress, shall not be denied or abridged by the United States or any State by reason of failure to pay any poll tax or other tax.

SECTION 2. The Congress shall have power to enforce this article by appropriate legislation.

AMENDMENT XXV

SECTION 1. In case of the removal of the President from office or of his death or resignation, the Vice President shall become President.

SECTION 2. Whenever there is a vacancy in the office of the Vice President, the President shall nominate a Vice President who shall take office upon confirmation by a majority vote of both Houses of Congress.

SECTION 3. Whenever the President transmits to the President pro tempore of the Senate and the Speaker of the House of Representatives his written declaration that he is unable to discharge the powers and duties of his office, and until he transmits to them a written declaration to the contrary, such powers and duties shall be discharged by the Vice President as Acting President.

SECTION 4. Whenever the Vice President and a majority of either the principal officers of the executive departments or of such other body as Congress may by law provide, transmit to the President pro tempore of the Senate and the Speaker of the House of Representatives their written

AMENDMENT 24. POLL TAXES OUTLAWED (1964)

A poll tax is a tax people must pay in order to vote. Some states used poll taxes to prevent poor people (mainly African Americans) from voting.

SECTION 1. The federal government and the state governments can't require people to pay a tax before voting in primary elections or for the President, Vice President, Senators, or Representatives.

SECTION 2. Congress can make laws to enforce this amendment.

AMENDMENT 25. THE ORDER OF SUCCESSION TO THE PRESIDENCY (1967)

SECTION 1. The Vice President will become President if the President dies, resigns, or is removed from office.

SECTION 2. The President will nominate a new person to be Vice President if the position becomes vacant. The nominee will become Vice President with the majority approval of both the House of Representatives and the Senate.

SECTION 3. The Vice President will become Acting President when the President informs the President Pro Tempore of the Senate and the Speaker of the House of Representatives that he is unable to fulfill his duties. The Vice President will remain Acting President until the President gives the President Pro Tempore and the Speaker of the House a written statement saying that he's fit to resume office.

SECTION 4. The Vice President will immediately become Acting President when the Vice President and a majority of the cabinet secretaries, or other officials Congress designates by law, inform the President Pro Tempore of the Senate and the Speaker of the House of declaration that the President is unable to discharge the powers and duties of his office, the Vice President shall immediately assume the powers and duties of the office as Acting President.

Thereafter, when the President transmits to the President pro tempore of the Senate and the Speaker of the House of Representatives his written declaration that no inability exists, he shall resume the powers and duties of his office unless the Vice President and a majority of either the principal officers of the executive department or of such other body as Congress may by law provide, transmit within four days to the President pro tempore of the Senate and the Speaker of the House of Representatives their written declaration that the President is unable to discharge the powers and duties of his office. Thereupon Congress shall decide the issue, assembling within forty-eight hours for that purpose if not in session. If the Congress, within twenty-one days after receipt of the latter written declaration, or, if Congress is not in session, within twenty-one days after Congress is required to assemble, determines by two-thirds vote of both Houses that the President is unable to discharge the powers and duties of his office, the Vice President shall continue to discharge the same as Acting President; otherwise, the President shall resume the powers and duties of his office.

AMMENDMENT XXVI

SECTION 1. The right of citizens of the United States, who are eighteen years of age or older, to vote shall not be denied or abridged by the United States or by any State on account of age.

SECTION 2. The Congress shall have power to enforce this article by appropriate legislation.

Representatives in writing that the President is unable to fulfill his duties.

The President will resume office when the he informs the President Pro Tempore of the Senate and the Speaker of the House in writing that he's able to fulfill his duties. If the Vice President and a majority of the cabinet secretaries, or other officials Congress designates by law, deliver another written statement within four days to the President Pro Tempore of the Senate and the Speaker of the House that the President is unable to fulfill his duties, then Congress will meet within forty-eight hours to resolve the dispute. The Vice President will continue to be Acting President if two-thirds of both the Senate and House of Representatives agrees within twenty-one days that the President is unable to fulfill his duties. Otherwise, the President will resume office.

AMENDMENT 26. VOTING RIGHTS FOR YOUTH (1971)

SECTION 1. The United States and individual states can't take away or hinder the right of all citizens, who are at least eighteen years old, to vote because of their age.

SECTION 2. Congress can make laws to enforce this amendment.

AMENDMENT XXVII

No Law, varying the compensation for the services of the Senators and Representatives, shall take effect, until an election of Representatives shall have intervened.

AMENDMENT 27. CONGRESSIONAL SALARIES (1999)

Laws that change the salaries of Senators and Representatives will take effect only after the next Congressional elections.

THE
GETTYSBURG
ADDRESS

Many modern historians believe that the Gettysburg Address captures the essence of America better than any other document, even the Declaration of Independence. In fewer than three hundred words, Abraham Lincoln argued that the war between the North and the South was not just a civil war but also a war to determine whether democracy was a valid system of government. Skeptical Europeans followed the Civil War carefully, knowing that the outcome would determine whether people could govern themselves without an absolute ruler. Lincoln therefore urged listeners to continue fighting the war for the future of democracy and humanity, to prove that "government of the people, by the people, for the people, shall not perish from the earth."

Lincoln delivered the Gettysburg Address on November 19, 1863, during the middle of the Civil War to commemorate the Union's victory in the Battle of Gettysburg. At the time, few people paid attention to the speech; in fact, no original copy even exists, and the speech has survived thanks only to a reporter who took the time to transcribe it as he listened to Lincoln speak.

THE GETTYSBURG ADDRESS

Four score and seven years ago our fathers brought forth on this continent, a new nation, conceived in Liberty, and dedicated to the proposition that all men are created equal.

Now we are engaged in a great civil war, testing whether that nation, or any nation so conceived and so dedicated, can long endure. We are met on a great battlefield of that war. We have come to dedicate a portion of that field, as a final resting place for those who here gave their lives that that nation might live. It is altogether fitting and proper that we should do this.

But, in a larger sense, we cannot dedicate—we can not consecrate—we can not hallow—this ground. The brave men, living and dead, who struggled here, have consecrated it, far above our poor power to add or detract. The world will little note, nor long remember what we say here, but it can never forget what they did here. It is for us the living, rather, to be dedicated here to the unfinished work which they who fought here have thus far so nobly advanced. It is rather for us to be here dedicated to the great task remaining before us—that from these honored dead we take increased devotion to that cause for which they gave the last full measure of devotion—that we here highly resolve that these dead shall not have died in vain—that this nation, under God, shall have a new birth of freedom—and that government of the people, by the people, for the people, shall not perish from the earth.

ORIGINAL TEXT

THE GETTYSBURG ADDRESS

The term score means twenty. Four score and seven years is another way to say eighty-seven years (4 x 20 + 7).

Eighty-seven years ago, the founders of the United States created a new country on this continent based on the principles of freedom and the belief that all men are equal.

We are currently fighting a civil war to determine whether this country—or any country based on the principles of liberty and equality—can survive. We're meeting on a major battlefield of that civil war, and we have come to dedicate part of this battlefield as a burial ground for the people who gave their lives here so that the United States could survive. It's appropriate that we do this.

But, in a greater sense, we can't make this ground any more sacred because the brave men who fought here—both those who're living and those who're dead—have already made this place sacred. It's beyond our ability to add or take away from their sacrifice. The world won't notice anything that we say here, but history can't forget the sacrifices that these men made. It's our responsibility to finish what they started. It's our job to continue fighting the war so that these men didn't die in vain and that this country, under God, will be free once again. We must make sure that government of the people, by the people, and for the people won't ever disappear.

APPENDICES

THE ARTICLES
OF CONFEDERATION
VS. THE CONSTITUTION

THE ARTICLES OF CONFEDERATION	THE CONSTITUTION

DURATION

• 1777–1788	• 1789–present

LEGISLATIVE BRANCH (CONGRESS)

• Unicameral Congress	• Bicameral Congress
• Each state gets one vote in Congress	• Each state gets two votes in the Senate; representation and votes in the House of Representatives are assigned according to population
• Decisions require unanimous approval	• Decisions require two-thirds approval in both the House and the Senate
• Congress can: - Declare war and peace - Print money - Maintain an army and navy - Establish post offices - Govern U.S. territories - Resolve all disputes between the states	• Congress can: - Declare war and peace - Print money - Maintain an army and navy - Establish post offices - Govern U.S. territories - Regulate interstate trade - Borrow money and issue credit for the United States - Set and collect taxes - Control immigration

THE ARTICLES OF CONFEDERATION	THE CONSTITUTION

EXECUTIVE BRANCH (PRESIDENCY)

- N/A

- Strong President, who is also the commander in chief of the armed forces

- The President is elected via the Electoral College for a term of four years

- The President can:
  - Enforce laws passed by Congress
  - Veto laws passed by Congress
  - Send and receive ambassadors
  - Appoint judges

JUDICIAL BRANCH (COURTS)

- N/A

- Federal court system headed by the Supreme Court

- The federal courts can:
  - Review cases involving the laws of the Constitution and United States
  - Hear appeals cases that state courts have already heard
  - Resolve disputes between states

AMENDMENTS

- Amendments require unanimous approval of the representatives in Congress

- Amendments require three-fourths approval of the state legislatures or special state conventions

FUN FACTS ABOUT THE CONSTITUTION

- The Constitution is the oldest written constitution in the world and also the shortest.

- More than 10,000 amendments to the Constitution have been proposed, but only thirty-three have gone to the states for ratification. Of these, twenty-seven have been ratified.

- The word *democracy* isn't mentioned anywhere in the Constitution.

- James Madison was considered to be the "father of the Constitution." He kept a detailed journal during the Constitutional Convention in Philadelphia, supported ratification, wrote many of *The Federalist Papers*, and wrote the Bill of Rights.

- The first and last pages of the original Constitution are kept in the National Archives in Washington, D.C. At night, the document is lowered into a vault capable of surviving a nuclear attack.

- The Constitution was written at the Philadelphia Convention in complete secrecy.

- Eighty-one-year-old Benjamin Franklin was the oldest man to sign the Constitution. The youngest man was only twenty-six.

- All states sent delegates to the Constitutional Convention except for Rhode Island. Rhode Island was also the last state to ratify the document.

- Scholars aren't quite sure who actually wrote the Constitution, though many believe it was Pennsylvania delegate Gouverneur Morris.

- Three delegates refused to sign the Constitution because they disliked the government it would create.

- The Constitution has influenced the writers of almost every other written constitution in the world.

LANDMARK SUPREME COURT CASES

1803 *MARBURY V. MADISON*
The Court decided that the Judiciary Act of 1789 was unconstitutional. This ruling established the precedent of judicial review—the Court's ability to decide whether Congress's laws were legal according to the Constitution.

1810 *FLETCHER V. PECK*
The Court decided that the legislature of Georgia could not revoke contracts awarded by other state legislatures. This decision protected legal contracts and strengthened the power of the Supreme Court to overrule state laws.

1819 *MCCULLOCH V. MARYLAND*
The Court decided that Congress had the power to create a national Bank of the United States according to the "necessary and proper" clause of the Constitution. This decision gave more power to the federal government.

1819 *DARTMOUTH COLLEGE V. WOODWARD*
The Court upheld the right of private organizations to hold private contracts. The decision further protected legal contracts and strengthened the power of the Supreme Court to overrule state laws.

1821 *COHENS V. VIRGINIA*
The Court upheld a previous ruling by the supreme court of Virginia. This decision solidified the Court's power to review decisions made in lower courts and therefore strengthened the power of the federal government.

1824 *GIBBONS V. OGDEN*
The Court ruled that the state of New York couldn't award monopolies to companies engaged in interstate commerce. The Court reaffirmed that only the federal government

could regulate interstate commerce as outlined in the Constitution.

1857 *DRED SCOTT V. SANFORD*

The Court decided that the slave Dred Scott would not win his freedom upon crossing into a free state. The Court also ruled that Scott couldn't sue his master because slaves were property and not citizens. This decision angered northerners in the years leading up to the Civil War.

1896 *PLESSY V. FERGUSON*

The Court upheld racial segregation and the "separate but equal" doctrine by legalizing separate facilities for blacks and whites in both private and publicly owned places. This decision impeded racial equality for blacks.

1904 *NORTHERN SECURITIES COMPANY V. UNITED STATES*

The Court decided that the Northern Securities Company was an illegal monopoly and forced the company to break up into smaller, more competitive companies. This decision strengthened the federal government's right to regulate interstate commerce.

1908 *MULLER V. OREGON*

The Court set a limit on the number of hours female laborers could work every week. This decision was one of the Court's first rulings that protected the rights of laborers.

1919 *SCHENCK V. UNITED STATES*

The Court decided that the federal government could restrict Americans' right to free speech if the speeches constituted a "clear and present danger" to the government. The decision validated the Espionage Act of 1917 that made it illegal to speak out against the government and the war effort during World War I.

1954 *BROWN V. BOARD OF EDUCATION OF TOPEKA, KANSAS*
The Court ruled that segregated public schools were unconstitutional. The decision reversed the Court's previous ruling in *Plessy v. Ferguson* and overturned the "separate but equal" doctrine.

1963 *GIDEON V. WAINWRIGHT*
The Court decided that all defendants accused of committing serious crimes have the right to legal representation, even if the government has to pay for it.

1966 *MIRANDA V. ARIZONA*
The Court decided that police must tell people they are about to question that they have the right to remain silent, that anything they say can be used against them in court, and that they have the right to legal representation. These rights have become known as Miranda rights.

1973 *ROE V. WADE*
The Court decided that the right to privacy protects women's right to have an abortion and that fetuses have no constitutional rights of their own.

1974 *UNITED STATES V. NIXON*
The Court decided that Presidents must comply with federal court orders and hand over any evidence to be used in criminal trials. The decision prompted President Richard Nixon to resign out of fear that the House of Representatives would impeach him.

1978 *REGENTS OF THE UNIVERSITY OF CALIFORNIA V. BAKKE*
The Court decided that federally funded universities couldn't admit students on the basis of race alone because such policies illegally penalized nonminority students. The Court decided that race was merely one factor such universities could consider when admitting applicants.

1998 *CLINTON V. THE CITY OF NEW YORK*

The Court decided that the Line-Item Veto Act, which gave the President the power to veto specific lines of proposed laws rather than the entire law itself, was unconstitutional because it gave the President too much power. The decision sought to maintain the separation of powers embedded within the Constitution.

1999 *DEPARTMENT OF COMMERCE V. U.S. HOUSE OF REPRESENTATIVES*

The Court decided that the Census Bureau could not use statistical sampling methods to determine the number of people living in the United States and must count each individual person when deciding how many representatives each state has in the House of Representatives.

2000 *BUSH V. GORE*

The Court decided that a manual recount of ballots in the presidential election of 2000 were unconstitutional because there were no uniform evaluation standards. The decision effectively guaranteed victory to candidate George W. Bush.

FURTHER READING

AMAR, AKHIL REED. *America's Constitution: A Biography*. New York: Random House, 2005.

AMAR, AKHIL REED. *The Bill of Rights*. New Haven: Yale University Press, 2000.

BAILYN, BERNARD. *The Debate on the Constitution: Federalist and Antifederalist Speeches, Articles, and Letters During the Struggle Over Ratification, January to August 1788*. New York: Library of America, 1993.

BERKIN, CAROL. *A Brilliant Solution: Inventing the American Constitution*. New York: Harcourt, 2003.

CUNNINGHAM, NOBLE E. *Jefferson vs. Hamilton: Confrontations that Shaped a Nation*. Boston: Bedford/St. Martin's, 2000.

DAHL, ROBERT A. *How Democratic is the American Constitution?* New Haven: Yale University Press, 2003.

DAVIS, SUE and J. W. PELTASON. *Understanding the Constitution*. Belmont, CA: Wadworth, 2003.

FEINBERG, BARBARA SILBERDICK. *The Articles of Confederation: The First Constitution of the United States*. Minneapolis: Lerner Publishing, 2002.

HAMILTON, ALEXANDER, JAMES MADISON, and JOHN JAY. *The Federalist*. New York: Barnes & Noble, 2006.

MAIER, PAULINE. *American Scripture: Making the Declaration of Independence*. New York: Random House, 1998

MEESE, EDWIN, III, MATTHEW SPAULDING, and DAVID FORTE. *The Heritage Guide to the Constitution*. Washington, D.C.: Regnery Publishing, Inc., 2005

MORGAN, EDMUND S. *The Birth of the Republic: 1763–89*. Chicago: University of Chicago Press, 1993.

RAKOVE, JACK N. *Original Meanings: Politics and Ideas in the Making of the Constitution*. New York: Knopf Publishing, 1997.

GLOSSARY

amendment—An alteration or addition to the Constitution. There have been twenty-seven amendments made to the Constitution.

appellate jurisdiction—The Supreme Court's power to hear cases that lower state and federal courts have already heard.

bicameral legislature—A legislature with two deliberative chambers. Most state legislatures and Congress are bicameral legislatures; the Senate is the upper chamber in Congress and the House of Representatives is the lower chamber.

bill of attainder—A law that takes away individuals' civil rights or private property without a trial.

Bill of Rights—The first ten amendments to the Constitution that protect the rights of the people and reserve some powers to both the people and the state governments.

checks and balances—The concept that each branch of government should be able to check the powers of the other branches so that no single branch becomes more powerful than the others. Examples of checks and balances include presidential vetoes and the Supreme Court's power of judicial review to declare laws unconstitutional.

Corruption of Blood—The practice of punishing the family members of people accused of crimes.

electoral college—The group of special electors chosen to elect the president and vice president.

ex post facto law—A law that punishes people for acts they committed before those acts became illegal.

executive branch—The branch of government responsible for enforcing laws that Congress creates. In the United States, the executive is the president of the United States.

grand jury—A jury of twelve to twenty-three people that examines evidence and decides whether the accused has committed a crime and if there should be a criminal trial.

House of Representatives—The lower chamber of Congress consisting of 435 representatives who are elected every two years.

impeach—To formally accuse an elected public official of committing serious crimes.

judicial branch—The branch of government responsible for interpreting the laws that Congress creates. In the United States, the judicial branch consists of a system of federal courts headed by the Supreme Court.

jury—A group of twelve people who decide the guilt or innocent of accused persons standing trial.

legislative branch—The branch of government responsible for making laws. In the United States, the legislative branch is Congress.

original jurisdiction—The Supreme Court's power to hear cases that no other state or federal court has already heard.

poll tax—A tax people must pay in order to vote. The 24th Amendment outlaws poll taxes.

president pro tempore—A senator who runs the Senate when the vice president is absent.

ratify—To formally approve an amendment or treaty.

repeal—To cancel an amendment.

Senate—The upper chamber of Congress consisting of two representatives from each state. Senators serve six-year terms, and one-third of all senators are elected every two years.

separation of powers—The concept that the powers of government have and should be divided into different branches (the legislative branch, the executive branch, and the judicial branch) so that the government doesn't become too powerful.

Speaker of the House—The person in charge of the House of Representatives.

unicameral legislature—A legislature with only one deliberative body. Nebraska is the only state in the Union with a unicameral legislature.

veto—The president's official rejection of a law that Congress has passed.

warrant—A court order authorizing police to arrest a person or search or take his belongings.

INDEX

Index